When You Feel Like
SCREAMING

Help for Frustrated Mothers

Updated with bonus selections from
KETTERMAN ON KIDS:
ANSWERS TO THE QUESTIONS PARENTS ASK MOST

■ ■ ■

Pat Holt and
Grace Ketterman, M.D.

SHAW

WATERBROOK
PRESS

When You Feel Like Screaming
A SHAW BOOK
PUBLISHED BY WATERBROOK PRESS
2375 Telstar Drive, Suite 160
Colorado Springs, Colorado 80920
A division of Random House, Inc.

Please note that all mothers' names, other than the authors, have been changed
to protect their privacy.

ISBN 0-87788-935-X

Library of Congress Cataloging-in-Publication Data
Ketterman, Grace H.
    When you feel like screaming : help for frustrated mothers : updated with bonus
  selections from Ketterman on kids / Grace Ketterman and Pat Holt.—[Updated ed.]
        p. cm.
    Holt's name appears first on the earlier edition.
    Includes index.
    ISBN 0-87788-935-X (pbk.)
      1. Discipline of children. 2. Child rearing. I. Holt, Pat, 1943- II. Title.

HQ770.4.K48 2001
649'.64—dc21   00-047701

Printed in the United States of America
2001—First Edition

10 9 8 7 6 5 4 3 2 1

When You Feel Like
SCREAMING

With love and gratitude to the one who inspired this book,
and to all the precious children and mothers
who shared their thoughts and feelings with such honesty and candor

■   ■   ■

CONTENTS

PREFACE

As you read this book, you may feel somewhat remorseful—even guilty—for the way you act around your kids. It is *not* our purpose to heap such painful emotions on you, but we do hope to help you recognize the damage screaming can do to your children and to yourself.

As you become aware of the dangers, we challenge you to stop screaming at your kids and avoid the grieving aftermath. You *can* learn to get the attention of your children and to discipline them with gentle, firm control. Such control will help you to achieve the desired results without the emotional pain and scars that can damage both you and your children.

We do *not* promote permissiveness in child rearing. Nor do we advocate the saccharine sweetness and whiny patience that are neither honest nor effective. Your children will hear and heed you best when you speak clearly and firmly with short statements that are verified by the expression on your face and the tone of your voice. They combine to say to the child, "I say what I mean, and I mean what I say."

Perhaps you have never considered that the intensity resulting from anger and the fear created by uncontrolled screaming is a form of child abuse. But it is. It may be conscious or unconscious, but it affects your family relationships. We'd like to offer you hope and some practical suggestions. We believe you can and would like to do better. That's why we wrote this book.

ACKNOWLEDGMENTS

This book was written with the help and encouragement of so many people. We are grateful to our current editor, Joan Guest, for her enduring patience and consistent support. Joyce Farrell, our agent, believed in the project from the very start, and her enthusiasm never wavered.

Our deepest appreciation to our "Project Allies" Trudi Ponder and Liz George, who prayed this book to completion.

SCREAMING!

Screaming!
No mom wants to,
but every mother feels like it.
SCREAMING!
If they'd be good…
If only they'd obey.
SCREAMING!
If only they would listen…
If only… If only…

PART 1

————

WHEN YOU FEEL
LIKE SCREAMING

Dear Mother,

In preparation for a mothers' seminar some time ago, we asked 150 nine- to twelve-year-olds to answer anonymously two questions:

- What do you like most about your mother?
- What do you dislike most about your mother?

The answers were written without any further discussion.

Although the answers to the first question varied, the answers to the second did not. We were amazed. Almost every child used the phrase *her screaming*. Over and over again we read, "I can't stand it when she screams."

Recently we went into six fourth-, fifth-, and sixth-grade classrooms and told the children we needed their help in writing a book for mothers. We wrote "Mommy, please stop screaming!" on the chalkboard, and knowing giggles and sighs of understanding followed. Two hundred children knew exactly what "Mommy, please stop screaming!" was about. Some of their stories are shared in this book so that we mothers can fully understand how our children see us and how our screaming affects them.

Mothers already know children "can't stand" screaming, and yet we continue to scream. Why? When? What are the factors that drive mothers to lose control?

We conducted a nationwide survey to answer these questions. The results of the survey and the responses of the mothers we interviewed are included in this book. The answers of these mothers demonstrate that regardless of the ages of the children, or the marital, professional, or socioeconomic status of the mothers, the reasons for screaming are the same.

Screaming is a habit, a habit that can be broken. Although the "screaming habit" breeds guilt in the mother, it can be difficult to break because many mothers are comfortable with the screaming (which usually guarantees a certain measure of success) and tolerate the guilt that follows.

Why is it so hard to develop new behavior patterns? Because changing behavior always involves risk. In the case of screaming, mothers risk leaving the comfort of the familiar habit with its predictable results for the unknown benefits of quiet control. The risk creates fearful anxiety, and anxiety makes the change difficult to attempt.

However, alternatives to screaming give such a high rate of success to the mother that her confidence level rises with continued use. Each successful experience will help the mother chip away at the wall of fear that keeps her from the personal confidence that ensures quiet control of herself and her children. Strong, controlled, confident women are capable and understanding mothers who raise confident and controlled children. We believe true strength is expressed only through gentleness and self-control. We look forward to journeying together with you in this book—to make you the best mother you can be.

Yours for keeping joy in motherhood,

Pat Holt and Grace Ketterman, M.D.

■ ■ ■

CHAPTER 1

WHEN YOU

LOSE CONTROL

I met Kathleen* in the hallway. She was an attractive and intelligent woman in her early forties and a business executive for a large corporation. She whisked me into her office and promptly shut the door. Then she began to tell me her story, with tears brimming in her eyes.

"I've alienated my children with my screaming," she cried. "My eighteen-year-old left home, my sixteen-year-old is there as little as possible, and when he is home all we do is scream at each other. My fourteen-year-old withdraws. I can't communicate with her at all. And the younger ones—well, I'm losing them, too." Her voice trailed off.

I discovered that this woman had a history of severe hormonal imbalances that caused excessive mood swings. She was under treatment that had considerably modified her behavior. Yet she still screamed; it was a habit. She'd done it for years. Why? Are the children really so terrible?

"It's my husband," she sobbed. "I get so frustrated with him. After twenty years of disappointment, I can't stand it anymore. Then I lash out at my children, especially if I see them display any of his irresponsibility."

How do the children react? They turn away from her, even when she tries to explain and defend herself. "They see my husband as the long-suffering hero," she complained.

Let's take a look at the facts in this situation. What are they? First,

---

* All names, except for the authors' names, have been changed to maintain privacy.

the mother screams. Why does she scream? For three reasons: because of her frustration with her husband that has been compounded through the years, because she worries that her children may become "irresponsible" like her husband, and because of her physical condition.

How does this screaming affect her relationships with her family? The children she loves have turned away from her. Her screaming also causes her children to overlook the father's faults and possibly to emulate them.

What are the results of screaming in her life? She feels alienated and guilty. As her frustration grows more intense, what happens? She continues to scream.

What this lady described is a vicious cycle. She screams out of frustration, feels guilty because she has screamed, then does not know what to do about the guilt, and thus feels even worse. The worse she feels, the more she screams, and so the cycle gains control over her. It starts to destroy her and her relationships. Unless the harmful screaming pattern is broken, the damage resulting from the uncontrolled rage will scar future generations.

This is exactly what happened in Kent's troubled family. Kent's mother screamed all the time. Not more than a day or two went by without his mother yelling at her five children. Kent lived in dread of her intense anger at even the slightest misdeeds. In fact, she even had screaming fits for which he could find no reason at all.

His mother also abused him physically. On one occasion, when he retorted rudely to his mother's yelling, she yelled even more. Then she told him she would whip him. Having had contact with her leather whipping strap before, Kent knew he wanted none of that, so he fled to the home of some new neighbors. He convinced them to let him spend the night. But time only fed the flames of his mother's fury. When he returned the next day, she greeted him with the strap and a stick.

Kent has never forgotten the pain of his punishments, the humiliation, helplessness, the fear and rage. They remain as emotional scars. He has tried to understand his mother, to forgive her, and to rise above the hurts her screaming inflicted, and so have the other children. But all of them have difficulty in their personal lives. There have been numerous divorces, and their children have suffered the fallout from their grandmother's rage.

Certainly Kent's mother was acting out the injustices of her own childhood. She screamed out of personal bitterness about needs that had never been met. She tried in unsuccessful ways to meet those needs, and then took out her pain and frustration on her helpless children.

No mother decides to be a screamer when she is holding her first precious newborn tenderly in her arms. So why do mothers scream? When does life become so frustrating that mothers lash out at their children in this way?

Through our study and experience we can pinpoint seven major situations that often result in screaming. Let's look at these together.

WHEN STRESS BECOMES TOO GREAT

Mothers scream when stress becomes too great. Listen to Mary's story:

> My first mistake was choosing the day after school let out to start painting my kitchen. Next, I agreed to baby-sit a friend's six-year-old for the same week. My husband had been working over-time for about a year, so most of the family responsibilities fell on me. In the middle of this, we got a call from my husband's eighty-one-year-old grandmother saying she would like to come spend the summer with us. It seemed like a good idea at the time. I was also getting the last plans worked out for Vacation Bible School for which I was the superintendent. I think if that was all that happened, I would have been fine, but that's not life.
>
> We received another phone call. A favorite uncle of mine was dying. I tried to "handle" everything myself. The next day I stood in the living room and screamed at my children—wanting to hit them. Now I don't even remember what they did.

Had this mother been able to say no to the excessive demands and needs of others, she would probably not have reached the screaming breaking point. Children are a mother's dearest and most important responsibility, next to her husband. You must be careful to reserve your best for them and give to others whatever time and energy is left.

Let's face it, however. This may be easy to say, but it is extremely difficult to put into practice. Nevertheless, attempting to "do it all"—cramming too much into a day, a week, or a season—will result in stress overload. A mother must learn to say no to the needs of others when the needs of her family will be endangered by her saying yes.

WHEN THERE ARE TOO MANY DEMANDS ON LIMITED TIME

Mothers scream when they have too much to do in a limited time. Trish, another busy mom, talks about the times she is most likely to scream:

> When I am late for an appointment or for work and there have already been endless interruptions from the telephone, my husband, and from the children. Then, as I am struggling to get the children to school on time, one of them tells me he forgot his lunch, homework, or whatever, and the other tells me she needs such and such for school today. Then I EXPLODE!

Preventing this sort of an explosion demands that a mother plan ahead. Getting up a little earlier, doing some food preparation the night before, and delegating duties to family members can work wonders in avoiding the frantic morning rush, as well as other stressful time periods.

Remember, also, that through countless other times of pressure, you have made it. Knowing you will succeed again can help keep you calm and prevent screaming.

Too often an unwelcome, unnecessary incoming phone call slows mothers down and ruins a perfectly good morning, afternoon, or evening schedule. Mothers can learn to avoid the "tyranny of the tele-phone." Some mothers refuse to be subject to the tyrant telephone and just don't answer the phone during peak crisis periods of the day. Their attitude is, "If it's important, they will call back or leave me a message!"

Mothers who are exceedingly curious or who must know who is calling for personal or business reasons should have voice mail, an answering machine, or a private answering service. It will save nerve strain and help them gain control of their time.

Other mothers train their children, as soon as they are accountable, to answer the phone and take a message. For younger children, this may be verbal. Older children can be responsible to take written messages. This book might never have been completed if Pat's children did not answer the phone and say, "She is not available right now. May I take a message?" They learned to say this at an early age and have been doing it consistently ever since. This particular wording works well—whether the mother is at home or away.

WHEN MOM DOESN'T FEEL WELL

Mothers scream when they do not feel well physically. Janet remembers a time when she screamed for this reason:

> It was a difficult premenstrual time for me. My fourteen-year-old had been home sick the week before finals and had not opened a book. Since she is not a good student, she needs to study hard to make average grades. I had gone to a lot of trouble to get her books and assignments for her. She had a lot to do! Well, Saturday she felt much better, put on her swimsuit, and was going to sit in the sun to get a tan. She had NO plans to open a book! I exploded!

While premenstrual tension is well known to most women, few know that they can do something about it. Believe you can control yourself even during those difficult days. Watch your calendar! When those days draw nigh, monitor your diet carefully, avoiding salt that can make your body retain more fluids. This will help take away the "beached blimp" feeling that makes you even more tense and irritable. For some people, indulgences in sweets, especially chocolate, also aggravate unpleasant symptoms. Talk to your physician about other remedies if your premenstrual symptoms are severe.

Mothers have a lot of demands on their time, and it's easy for them to get run-down physically. This makes them susceptible to the colds and other illnesses that children bring home from school. Headaches, back-aches, colds, flu, and all sorts of aches and pains assail us.

When you feel ill or suffer from the tensions of PMS, listen to your body—it is warning you! Plan a lighter schedule if at all possible. Get extra rest. Simplify your life and say no when your emotional health is on the line. Avoid weighty decisions. Whenever possible, postpone decision making until you feel better. You'll be glad you did. Take more time than usual to handle personal and family situations. Do *not* give an ultimatum based on hormonal imbalance!

There are many physical problems that can make your discomfort level high and your patience short. Take good care of yourself—you deserve it. This is good preventive medicine for busy moms. If and when you are ill, learn to simplify your life, organize your family to help, and practice special self-control so you will not feel worse from remorse than from your illness.

Sounds easy, you say. But you know it's hard in real life. You struggle with it. Just how do we go about simplifying and organizing? Don't despair. We'll look at some practical solutions in the next chapters.

When Mom Feels Helpless

Mothers scream when they feel helpless. Evelyn, a twenty-six-year-old single mother, expresses her frustration:

I am a single parent. My worst day came three weeks ago. My employer told me I would not be needed as of the first of the month. My son's teacher told me that he continually disrupts the classroom, is aggressive on the playground, and just tried to forge my signature on a failing paper. Driving home in the rain, I got a flat tire, and no one stopped to help. About this time, my son asked if he could have a candy bar. That did it. I screamed longer and harder than I ever have in my life!

Remember the proverbial straw that broke the back of the unsuspecting camel? That is a truth for mothers to consider: to avoid the relentless buildup of frustration that will allow one small thing—like a child's asking for candy—to set off an explosion. When you suffer under the weight of pressures you must re-establish equilibrium. How can you do this? As one stress hits, deal with it instantly. Dealing with it means accepting the stress—*not* denying its existence. Find out what you can do about the stress, decide who can help you with it, and set a specific time when you will put the plan in motion. Then put that stress out of your mind. This will not eliminate the things that cause stress, but such planning will help you deal with them as they come along instead of letting them build up. It will also make you aware of your real strength and how to make that strength work for you.

Of course, Evelyn had several major stressors dumped on her that one day that weren't things that could be dealt with immediately and set aside. But she could deal with the emotional impact. For example, she received the news that she was losing her job. She needed to take a time out, quiet her emotions and pray about this news. Then maybe she could call or e-mail a couple of friends and ask to talk with them that evening to begin thinking through her next move. Then she could consciously put the job situation out of her mind, and perhaps she would have been more ready to hear the news from her son's teacher. That could have been handled immediately by asking for an appointment with the teacher to discuss the issues further. Even these big stressors can be dealt with a little at a time leaving moms with more emotional energy to cope with their "little" stressors—the children.

WHEN HER CHILDREN DON'T SEEM TO MEASURE UP

Mothers scream when their children don't seem to be measuring up to their wishes or expectations. Terri, a vivacious thirty-year-old, told me this story:

> A particular instance is written in my mind as if it were yester-day. On my doorstep appeared an outraged neighbor with her three-year-old boy who had a very red, long, ugly mark on his back. The mother raked me over the coals because my five-year-old son had hit her son. She was so angry. I was stunned by her outburst and had nothing to say.
>
> When I finally closed the door, I went after my son. He knew he was never to hit children, and so, without giving him a chance, I let him have it, screaming incessantly to vent my anger and disappointment. I was so mad. I never asked to hear his side of the story.

That story reminds Grace of the years she lived under the ugly cloud of others' expectations, feelings, and opinions of her and her children. It was a great day when she learned that her children were her first consideration. She found out how to explore with them what had really happened. Often they were not the only ones at fault. She learned to discipline more wisely and *much* more effectively when she discovered the value of listening instead of reacting without thinking. More on that later.

WHEN HER CHILDREN REMIND HER
OF SOMEONE WHO HURT HER

Mothers scream when their children consciously or unconsciously remind them of a difficult someone in their lives, someone who has hurt them. Jan admitted,

> You'd better believe I scream when my ten-year-old son shows any of the characteristics of the man who sired him, lied to me, and abandoned both of us in the hospital. I never want to see a trace of that man in my son!

This mother's words graphically illustrate the crucial need to work through every troubled relationship. Forgiveness and healing are absolute necessities. Few families have no bothersome people in them. When a child has the misfortune to resemble that problem person, it is very easy to displace bad feelings toward another person onto that child. Not only does the child suffer the consequences of his own misdeeds, he also suffers the results of old bitterness toward someone else. We will deal with the essential role of forgiveness in possessing a healthy emotional life and, specifically, in controlling screaming, in chapter 8.

WHEN MOM FEARS HER CHILDREN
MAY GO WRONG

Mothers scream when they fear their children may not grow up to be what or who they "should" be.

One mother screamed regularly at her seven children. Her daughter Nancy recalls, "I dreaded her screamed-out lectures more than a spanking! Even now I can hear her shrill voice, disapproving manner, and endless flow of words. I tried extremely hard to gain her approval, but I rarely felt I merited it." While this mom's screaming encouraged them to achieve, it instilled loads of self-doubt.

WHEN MOM DOESN'T SCREAM

From our study, we know not only when mothers are *most* likely to scream, but when they are *least* likely to scream.

One extremely frustrated mother said that she is least likely to scream when "everyone is asleep." Another told us, "I am least likely to scream when I have laryngitis!" Those familiar truths brought us all a chuckle.

The majority of mothers that we interviewed, however, are least likely to scream when

- they are rested,
- things are calm,
- the children cooperate without complaint,
- they are "getting things done,"
- there are other people around.

Because life is seldom ideal, mothers do scream. But there is hope. We have discovered that why mothers scream, what they verbalize, and the type of fundamental love and acceptance they express toward their children make all the difference.

We believe you and your children will *feel* better and *do* better when you master different disciplinary skills. And that's what we'd like to share with you in the coming chapters of part 1 of this book.

■ ■ ■

CHAPTER 2

FOR REASONABLE REASONS

"I want to be heard so very badly because I care for my children. I love them so much and want the best for them. If it takes volume to get the message across, that's what I use. I do what I have to do to get the message across."

These words are echoed by mothers all over the nation. It is ironic that the very results mothers yearn for fall short because they make a costly mistake—the mistake of screaming. The problem is that screaming *seems* to work. It certainly gets the children's attention, though it takes ever-increasing volume to do it.

However, the lasting effect of screaming is that psychological calluses form on the eardrums. Louder and louder volume is demanded to obtain the desired result. After a while, even screaming doesn't penetrate the wall that screaming has set up in the relationship between parent and child.

Of the many reasons mothers give for *why* they scream, nine stand out. We'll take them one at a time.

IT GETS THEIR ATTENTION

Why do many mothers scream? Just to get their children's attention. Mandy often feels exasperated with her son:

When I speak to my thirteen-year-old son in a normal tone of voice, he doesn't even hear. It doesn't matter what I am saying. I usually repeat my request five or six times, and then I scream, "I'm talking to you—get over here!"

His general attitude is that of disgust. He feels that I'm intruding into his reverie, or television program, etc. He is rarely doing his homework at times like this.

Of course, when he finally grants me his attention, he answers, to whatever it is, "I can't now. I'm doing my homework."

This makes me even more irritated, and I scream, "You've had four hours to do it!" etc.

Then he sighs a big sigh and throws down his pencil. "Oh, all right," he says grudgingly and slowly limps in my direction.

This boy is not likely to do whatever it is his mother asks. He sounds angry, and his mother recognizes he is disgusted. Perhaps that feeling is due to her intrusion, but we suspect it is aggravated by the *way* she intrudes.

At thirteen, he is beginning to feel like a man and needs to be treated more like one. Enduring Mom's yelling may remind him of his early years. He may resent being treated like a child. How can you treat an adolescent with respect for his time and interests and yet get the job done? Here are a few tips.

- The mother needs to talk with the boy as an individual rather than as his commander. Respect for his schedule includes giving him a broad base of time in which to accomplish the task she requests. That way, she demonstrates respect for whatever it is he is doing, whether she approves of the expenditure of time or not. If he has a voice in deciding when he will do assigned tasks, he is far more likely to cooperate.

- If at the end of the agreed-upon time the task is not completed, consequences must follow. Since both agreed on the work to be done, the consequences become the choice of the boy rather than an infliction from the mother. The consequences should be determined by what is important to the boy at his stage and also should be commensurate to his age.

VOLUME WILL DRIVE THE MESSAGE HOME

Mothers hope that increased volume will get the point across more clearly, that it will make their children understand the message. Sarah, a mother of five, felt that way:

> My ten-year-old daughter does not hear me unless I am in a higher decibel range. When I get her attention at long last, I speak clearly, firmly, and louder than usual. I always end with, "Do you understand me?" I do this to draw some kind of a response. Then I can always say later, "When we talked about this before, you said you understood."

Screaming does not enhance a child's understanding. In fact, a child almost always associates loudness with anger. For children, and adults as well, anger produces fear or anxiety. And fear commonly blocks learning. While the child may agree that she understood, it may well be that she agreed in order to prevent further screaming. The important point the mother wants to make may be lost entirely. Exasperating, isn't it?

One nurse in a children's hospital has a very different means of getting a message home to a noisy, unheeding child. She draws the child close to her and whispers in his ear. Few children can resist wanting to hear a secret, and even the most troublesome child stops resisting, listens, and complies with her quiet request.

IT GETS RESULTS

Most mothers recognize that when they scream, their children get moving. Brenda realized she used screaming to set fires under her slow-moving children.

> My daughters needed to eat lunch quickly and go to ballet. I told my nine-year-old to cover up her clothes in case she spilled. Of course she spilled her entire lunch over her leotard, then sauntered over to the sink to clean up. "Wipe it up thoroughly. We must get going!" Still slow action. I turned up the volume —"GET MOVING!"—and got results.
>
> My eleven-year-old daughter was sitting barefoot at the table, half-consciously picking at her food without making any headway. Time was a consideration, so in order to get action I turned up the volume. "Move, kid!" That sent her flying out the door, socks in mouth, and a shoe in each hand. Not nastiness but the vocal push helped the go-cart go!

Screaming is not *always* bad. In an emergency it will produce action. The problem with yelling habitually, however, is that of the proverbial shepherd boy who loudly and habitually cried "Wolf!" to get the attention and comfort of other people. When a wolf really appeared no one believed him, and no one came to the rescue.

Screaming stimulates nervousness in children. We know that a parent's irritation can be a factor in spilling and breaking things. Children may actually slow to a standstill because they dread the next level of Mom's anger. Understandably enough, moms see this as stubbornness or even defiance. Perhaps remembering how you felt as a child when someone yelled at you can help you understand your child better.

Logically, a child should get moving toward compliance to avoid repeated yelling. But the child's emotions interfere with logical thinking. If you want to stop screaming and yet gain your child's obedience and respect, put yourself in her shoes. If you felt as she does, what would work? How would you learn to give those desired results? Then try out your own new ideas! You may discover some wonderful techniques that really work for you and your child.

IT SHOWS THEM HOW THEIR BEHAVIOR AFFECTS ME

Many mothers are just trying to help their children understand how much their behavior affects them. Gini felt that way.

> My daughter was two and a half years old and in the middle of potty training. I was eight months pregnant and feeling very tired and immobile. I was worn out from trying to meet my daughter's physical needs. I had used all the encouraging words. Finally I couldn't physically keep up with her demands. "Go to the bathroom now, honey. You can do it." She wouldn't go. She stood there in front of me, arms folded, and wet her pants through everything. I knew it was defiance. I became furious and made her sit in her own puddle until I could cool down. I did more than a reasonable amount of screaming!

One of the negative results of regular screaming is the creation of a wall of resentment between mother and child. The resentment is mixed with anxiety, and young children have no words for expressing these profound, often intense, feelings. They are left to act them out in one of two ways: They become aggressive or hyper and begin yelling themselves, or they withdraw in silent resistance. Often they role-play their responses while playing with other children.

At no age, perhaps, is this more evident than the twos. The mother of a two-year-old who struggles with the screaming habit would be wise to postpone potty training for a while. Even though there would be extra work involved, both the mother and her child would be far better off in the long run. The toilet-training process might have been much less stressful for Gini and her daughter if Gini had waited until after she had the baby and was more comfortable physically. They could probably have avoided the emotional barrier building of Mom's anger. That little girl would learn to use the potty in due time.

It is important for children to understand how parents feel, but it is even more important that the children do not feel guilty for causing a parent's bad feelings. Gini saw her daughter's seemingly deliberate wetting as a personal attack on her. The physical discomfort and the pressure to toilet train her child before the arrival of a new baby pushed her to her breaking point. The combination of factors, not the two-year-old, unleashed her angry screaming.

Although she screamed, Gini wisely chose to take time to cool down before she took action. That cooling-down time can be a lifesaver. Discipline yourself to think about all the facts and feelings in any tense situation. Avoiding blame will help you handle life more effectively.

It Makes Me Feel Better

When mothers scream, it releases the building anger and frustration—for the moment. Mary Lou, a homemaker and part-time data processor, shared this with me:

> Maybe I am unique in this area, but I am deeply affected by behaviors such as irresponsibility and undependableness. They go against my nature. When I see my children displaying such behavior, or leaning in this direction, I try to say to myself, *They're not like me. I need to accept them as they are.* But it doesn't work. Sooner or later I scream, and it does make me feel better because I'm so frustrated. I'm venting my frustration in the sense that when I scream at my children about irresponsibility, I am really yelling at my husband, "You are allowing this thing to

happen. You are allowing mediocrity, and I cannot accept this. I don't want the children to turn out like you."

Some mothers feel much better after screaming. But sooner or later, they yell again—proof that the good feeling does not last. So don't let that temporary good feeling deceive you! We hope to help you find lasting joy and peace of mind in your parenting skills.

It is especially devastating to children to feel that one parent criticizes or puts down the other. When the child's misbehavior is likened to the "bad" parent's, that child experiences an upheaval of emotions. The child is hurt by and angry with the yelling parent. The child fears he is no good and that the other parent is no good either. The child believes he is doomed to become an adult who is "bad like Dad," so he feels hopeless and helpless. Anger, sadness, guilt, fear, and helplessness are the well-defined ingredients of depression. This price tag for a mother to feel temporarily better after screaming is simply too high.

There are successful ways to help your children become fine adults. Your disappointments and frustrations regarding their dad will have to be worked out. Please refer to chapter 8 on forgiving. There is great hope for you!

IT'S BETTER THAN HITTING THEM

Mothers who scream because it is better than hitting are correct—screaming *is* better than hitting their children. This was something that Angie, a shy forty-year-old, struggled with.

> I've been responsible for my stepdaughter since she was four
> years old. To the best of my ability, I have always been available
> to give her motherly love and advice. Her father adores her. On
> one particular occasion during her teen years, we had taken her
> on a trip. She was glad to take everything we offered, but when

her dad wanted her to go somewhere with him, she wasn't interested because she wanted to spend time with a boy.

I tried to support her father by pointing out to her that we had indulged her every whim and that she should do something for her father. I felt strong rejection from her, and she screamed, "I don't have to listen to you! You're not my mother!"

I couldn't take any more, and so I screamed back, "I'm glad I'm not your mother!" Believe me, I felt like hitting her!

Getting out one's frustrations by screaming rather than hitting is commendable! Child abuse is a tragedy—it affects the lives of so many families in a destructive way. But we have good news for you. You do not need to resort to either hitting *or* yelling. There are other choices.

In this situation, the stepmother and father needed to work together. The facts seem to indicate that Dad, who adores her, may unwittingly have pampered his daughter. Most mothers rightfully resent such spoiling, but out of love and respect for their husbands (or helplessness to open his eyes!) they keep quiet and take their resentment out on the child.

Rather than yelling or hitting, this stepmother and dad could have asked for a few minutes alone. A calm, clear statement from Mother reflecting this girl's ingratitude and selfish, demanding ways might have opened Dad's eyes. Out of concern for this girl's future relationships and character, they could have come up with a plan to help her. Grounding her for the evening from all fun could have taught her a much-needed lesson. Mom and Dad could have had a nice time, and almost certainly this daughter would behave better next time.

I LEARNED IT FROM MY MOTHER

Many mothers, either consciously or unconsciously, struggle in a cycle of abuse learned during their childhood. Can you identify with Tina?

My mother was a screamer, and looking back it seems to me that all she ever did was yell at my sister and me. Now both of us have children of our own. One thing we never wanted to do was be like her, and yet it has happened. Our children call us "The Screaming Duet." We feel like such utter failures. I can't believe we've turned out to be just like that woman.

In chapter 1, we described Kent's mother and her screaming pattern. His sister revealed that, to her horror she, too, yelled at her children. Every time she did, she ended up in tears of remorse with painful memories of her childhood. She worked heroically to break that habit and was able to find more successful means to train her children.

SCREAMING SEEMS POWERFUL

Many mothers told us that screaming made them feel powerful. Susan sat across from us at McDonalds. As we ate our burgers, we chatted about our children and the frustrations we felt. She hung her head and focused intently on her fries as she said:

Most of the time my child-rearing efforts seem futile. Usually I accept being taken for granted and am rather passive. But on certain occasions, with enough provocation, I get very angry and really let the children have it. Perhaps I shouldn't admit this, but I get a sense of power that comes with my anger and my screaming at those times.

Raising children properly in today's stressful times is not easy. When too many burdens pile up on you, you may fear that you just can't cope. You are likely to feel inept, weak, or inadequate. It is extremely likely that you will discover a sense of power when you yell. That feeling seems much more desirable than those negative emotions. Before you realize it, you can develop the screaming habit.

Remember our philosophy: True strength is always gentle—and real gentleness is strong.

I FEEL DESPERATE

Some mothers scream because they reach a desperation point. Carrie, who got married at eighteen, talked about her marriage and family.

> Nothing has turned out the way I planned. I had the same hopes and dreams every little girl has of being pursued by Prince Charming, getting married, and living happily ever after. Instead I settled for a weakling, supported him through school, had the children, took care of him and the children, and then was left when he got tired of "all the responsibility." Yes, I scream. I scream at shattered and broken dreams.

Any mother can feel desperate, but those who are especially vulnerable to that extreme condition are single moms. They heroically struggle to maintain a home by working long hours and then facing all of the demands of child rearing alone. Among those who are divorced, only a few have resolved the hurts and anger left from the divorce, and many times the mannerisms of their children remind them of their ex-husbands.

The personal losses of a marriage, financial support, and social position, plus the immense responsibilities that must now be shouldered alone combine to create nearly impossible living conditions. It is necessary to find some support if you are to avoid taking out your frustration on your children.

If you will look around, you will find many moms who suffer from nearly identical problems. They need support too. We suggest you find other single mothers and plan creatively some means of alternating childcare now and then to permit some personal time for each mother. Assisting each other with budgeting, hearing solutions others have discovered, and occasionally allowing time simply to communicate can take the edge off your stress. You will find it far more possible to be firm, consistent, and reasonable with your children if you enjoy this sort of support system.

You may have a reason for yelling that we haven't discovered. Whatever the reason, we believe it's not good enough to excuse your continuing to scream. As you read on, you will learn how children react to mothers' screaming and why you need to find another method to get them to do what you want them to do.

■ ■ ■

CHAPTER 3

BUT IT'S AFFECTING

YOUR CHILDREN

There is a wide disparity between how parents *believe* their children react to their screaming and how the children actually respond. Mothers do not want their children to think of their yelling or screaming in a negative way.

> I was devastated to discover that my children thought that I screamed a lot. Perhaps it is just that they take my screaming more seriously than I intend. I wish that they could understand screaming is not just a way of getting my point across but is also my way of venting pent-up frustration.

This parent feels her yelling serves two purposes: It gets her point across, and it vents her pent-up frustration. It would be nice if children could understand adults better. When mothers take time to explain their moods and yelling to children, it helps; but children who are hurt, afraid, or anxious cannot get beyond themselves to comprehend the entire situation. It is unrealistic to expect them to understand emotions that adults themselves have difficulty handling.

To a child, screaming is like a cancer. When that screaming enters a child's ears, it quickly spreads, killing the child's fragile cells of growing self-esteem. Without healthy self-esteem, the child cannot achieve his or her God-given potential and will become increasingly anxious, insecure, and often angry.

We urge you moms who are habitual screamers to try to explain your feelings to your children. When you are not upset and can remain calm, take time to talk together. Tell them you are anxious to teach them responsibility, good behavior, and excellence in how they do their work. Help them understand that at times you get worried that you aren't doing as good a job as you'd like and then you find yourself screaming to *make* them respond. You may, of course, have a different explanation, but interpreting your actions will help your children respect you and enable them to be less hurt when you do scream.

Unfortunately, the emotional distress that children experience is not the only result of a mother's screaming. Like it or not, children learn from example and will emulate what they hear and observe. A screaming mother signals to the young child that screaming is an acceptable form of communication, and all too soon the child begins to respond by screaming back. This screaming chain is self-perpetuating, and it becomes a highly developed and unfortunate habit deeply ingrained in the personality of the child. Children respond to screaming in one or more of the following ways.

SADNESS AND HURT FEELINGS

Some children react to yelling with sadness. This fifth-grade student poignantly describes her sad and hurt response to her mother's yelling:

> It really breaks my heart when she yells or screams like that. I
> just wish she was not a yeller or screamer. I wish that she would
> be a little more tender and nice.

This child makes it very clear that Mom's screaming "breaks [her] heart." It is almost certain that *every* child feels pain at first when a mother screams. Through a variety of protective devices, children learn to stop hurting and adapt to the yelling over which they have no control.

Pain in any child will cause one of three responses:
- the child will withdraw and suffer the pain in silence;
- he or she will learn to cover the pain with a facade of indifference or anger; or
- he or she will likely escape from the mother emotionally and even physically.

We will discuss these reactions in more detail in this chapter.

ANGRY BACK TALK

Other children lash back at parents when they yell. A fourth-grade boy wrote this personal experience:

> Once my brother was playing the piano and he hit a wrong note and my mommy hit his hand. My brother said, "Mom, why did you do that?" My mommy said, "Because you hit a wrong note." So my mom screamed at my brother, and my brother screamed at my mommy. They went on screaming until my daddy got home. I think my brother felt mad. My mommy could have handled it better by saying, "Try another note" or by saying, "You touched one wrong note."

The child who wrote this story is requesting that his mother exercise more patience and self-control—an appropriate and logical request. But self-control in the heat of frustration is very difficult.

This mom screamed because her son's piano playing did not meet her expectations, and her son reacted by yelling back. Obviously he felt angry and resented her screaming. Sadly, the mother defeated her well-intentioned objective (helping her son learn and achieve) by the method she used (screaming). In fact, if this boy had really wanted to become a pianist, he may well have rebelled and failed to reach that goal because of the anger created by such screaming matches.

The ill will created by mothers' screaming extends into adult life, as the following story illustrates. Only recently, Helen, an adult daughter of a mother who screamed at her, returned to her hometown to visit her brothers. She decided that she would not visit her mother or even call her. Believing their mother would be hurt if her daughter failed to reach out to her, the brothers prevailed on her to phone their mom.

Helen had learned to scream at her own children and husband, and she hated this trait in herself as much as she had hated it in her mother. So when she called her mother, the two of them promptly engaged in an angry yelling match on the telephone. The mother accused, "I guess I just don't have a daughter anymore!" Pathetically, Helen screamed back, "Mom, there were plenty of times I felt I didn't have a mother!"

Helen illustrates several reactions to her mother's screaming— yelling back, drawing out fear and dread of the habitual anger, and leaving home early (she went to live with relatives as a young teenager).

Screaming, in the long run, has a painful, negative payoff.

FEAR AND WITHDRAWAL

Some children are sensitive and easily intimidated by others' intensity. They respond to anger and screaming by withdrawing. One such child's attempt to help his mother backfired.

> One night I tried to do the wash as a favor. But I didn't know what I was doing. My mom was upset and started to scream. Her best skirt was ruined. I think if she would have had more temperance she wouldn't have screamed. I felt like running away. I hid behind the dresser. But I came out because I was hungry.

This child states clearly that running away was a strong temptation. An adult friend, a victim of a yelling mother, told us that he, his sister, and his brother left home in their mid-teens. They did so because they could no longer tolerate what they experienced as abuse—their mother's screaming.

If you are a screaming mom and it seems to be working, reconsider! While your children may tolerate your yelling and even comply with your requests when you yell, they may be storing away the pain and resentment until they can escape it all. Look into the years ahead. If your child continues to react as he or she does now, what could happen to him or her ten years from now? Keeping that question in mind has often helped us to avoid screaming at our own children.

ANGRY, SULLEN SILENCE

Many children quickly identify an almost unbeatable weapon against a screaming mother: They ignore her in quiet, seething anger. The silence of anger is very different from that of sadness and hurt.

> I went to school once. I had a sandwich with mayonnaise and I
> hate mayonnaise and she knows it, so I didn't eat it. When I got
> home my mom screamed at me. I went to my room and
> ignored her for the rest of the day.

When a child yells back a verbal fight ensues in which neither child nor parent really wins. In such a fight, however, both express feelings and there is a certain equality of power, however negative it is.

But when a child withdraws into angry silence, the balance in the power struggle tips in the child's favor. The results are often tragic. Such silent anger sometimes increases a mother's anger and leads to abuse. A mother, desperate to win the combat, may resort to physical violence to "break the will" of her child. But instead she usually breaks her child's heart and the bonds that tie her child to her.

Every time I'm watching my favorite television show my mommie tells me to do chores. I asked her if I could do them later.
She has to scream, "Get in here young man and do your
chores!" I hate it when my mommie screams. It makes me feel
as if I am two inches tall. Just because she screamed she is in a
bad mood and when I get screamed at I'm in a bad mood.
Mommie please, stop screaming.

This child's story reveals a common combat zone between parents
and children—that of giving up pleasure and substituting work.
Mothers are correct in trying to teach their children to be responsible.
But screaming is not an appropriate teaching technique! Children are
likely to feel "two inches tall"—quite helpless and worthless. Good parenting demands building into children the qualities of worth, confidence, and respect. Prolonged efforts at instilling these traits into children can be undone by a few episodes of screaming which, for the
moment at least, made this child feel worthless.

HUMILIATION AND SHAME

Just as certain sensitive children react to mothers' screaming with fear,
others respond with humiliation and shame. The most serious, deep,
and painful humiliation and shame occur when a mother's yelling
comes in the presence of a friend. Both the child and his friend were
embarrassed in the following example.

My friend's mom is constantly screaming at him for no reason,
but sometimes he is bad like the time he threw a pail of water
over her head. When that happened, all she did was scream. I
don't know about him, but it made me feel uneasy. I think she
should be more calm. At least try. Then I think she should have
punished him because all screaming does is make him nervous
and not want to trust her anymore.

These humiliating experiences are more common than we like to think. Grace remembers one of her own:

I shall never forget one experience of shame from my own mother's yelling. When I was in the first grade, I was in the Christmas program at school. Dressed in our Sunday best, we were all lined up on the stage to sing Christmas carols for our parents and interested neighbors. Only one child among us wore new clothes, since that Christmas occurred in the depths of the Depression. This child stood beside me as we sang, and I became enchanted with the fuzzy yarn balls at the ends of the bow tied at the neck of her gorgeous golden sweater. Finally I could resist no longer. I reached over, not missing a note, and touched those delightfully soft miniature pom-poms.

The next morning, during breakfast, my mother lectured me resoundingly about my behavior. She told me that she had been embarrassed and that the entire audience had laughed. She went on at some length. When I could, I crept away and hid behind the kitchen stove. I doubt a criminal sentenced for a crime could feel worse than I did that day. Like the child in the other story, I did not want to trust her anymore.

Fortunately, there was a redemptive ending to that situation. My father left the table and searched until he found me. He lifted me up in his strong arms, looked at me with tender brown eyes, and said, "Gracie, I didn't think it was so bad! In fact, it was kind of cute!" Never again did he ever counter one of mother's screams, but that one time was enough to restore hope and even self-respect.

Mothers, let us make this a plea! Don't yell at your children in a way that robs them of the self-esteem that is so essential to the emotional health you want them to develop.

FORMING A COALITION AGAINST MOTHER

When mothers scream, children look to defend themselves. One mother says, "My children seem to gang up on me. If I only had to deal with one at a time, I'm sure I could do okay. But when all three of them get together, how can I cope with them?"

In this case, further investigation revealed a mom who sincerely wanted her children to become respectful, well-behaved people. Her methods of stretching for that goal, however, were responsible for their coalition of rebellion. She spoke loudly, threatened, and shamed the children, and did so openly in front of all of them. The victim looked to the others for sympathy and support and invariably received a wink or a gesture that met his needs. In turn, he gave similar sympathy to his sister and brother. As time went on, they became companions not only in punishment but also in new acts of mischief.

Mothers, please stop screaming. Find the time to take a child who needs correction to a place of privacy. Gain the self-control you need to explain what was wrong, how to correct it, and what you will do to help make the right things happen. We will discuss other corrective measures later.

INDIFFERENCE OR LAUGHTER

When children endure screaming frequently, they often learn to act as if they don't care. I have heard children say, "Mom, I've heard that lecture so many times, I know it by heart!" It seems that children develop an attention block so they actually do not hear their mothers' yelling. Such indifference, real or feigned, can further infuriate moms who are already upset!

One friend tells this truly remarkable story. Her mother was left alone a great deal because of her husband's work. She struggled to raise six children single-handedly, and she yelled a *lot* in the process.

This friend's little brother seemed to get more than his share of their mother's yelling. One day she really let him have it, and he stoically heard her out. He was only six, but when she finally became calm, this gentle child said, "Mommy, you really hurt my feelings when you yell, but I still love you"!

Whatever your child's reaction to your screaming may be, please consider stopping. The scars and calluses it creates in your child can be difficult—if not impossible—to erase.

■ ■ ■

CHAPTER 4

AFTER THE STORM

Episodes of screaming are always two-party encounters. We've discussed how *children* react to their mothers' screaming. Now we need to explore how *mothers* feel after screaming. When asked on the survey, most mothers replied with one of the four emotions we'll discuss in this chapter.

GUILT

Guilty is the self-imposed verdict of an overwhelming majority of mothers we questioned. When asked how they feel after a screaming session, again and again the mothers wrote, "Guilty."

As painful as guilt is, it serves a most useful purpose! In fact, because it is so painful, guilt is a powerful motivator for change. We were glad to discover that so many moms were honest enough to admit they feel guilty.

There are several reasons for this sense of guilt. These will help you understand yourselves and each other better. Through understanding comes forgiveness and the capacity to change your habits.

I Lost Control

The mothers in our study responded with many revealing comments about how they feel:

- My four-year-old doesn't deserve to be screamed at. He's hurt and confused, and I'm left guilty.

- I feel guilty and out of control. My twelve-year-old daughter will look at me as if to say, "Here she goes again," and plug her ears. She has also told me that I don't love her because I scream.
- I feel guilty that I have vented my frustration, but with no positive results.
- I feel guilty because it usually means I overreacted to the situation.
- I feel guilty because I allowed circumstances to control me.
- I feel terribly guilty. One Saturday I screamed so loud and long at my fourteen-year-old, it ruined our entire weekend. We all cried and cried. It took me three days to feel good about myself again. That day I apologized to everyone, asked for forgiveness, had a long talk with my daughter, prayed with her, etc. But only God can repair the damage I did to my relationship with her. I wounded her deeply. I feel like a total failure as a mom.

What Else Could I Do?

Mothers also feel guilty because they didn't change their behavior. One mom responded, "I feel guilty. I often wonder why I keep making the same mistakes instead of learning from them and becoming more effective in communicating quietly with my children."

I Feel So Inadequate

Moms who scream suffer consequences along with their children. It may permanently affect their sense of self-confidence in their mothering skills.

- I feel guilty and inadequate. I have usually said something I wish I hadn't—something that was an exaggeration of the problem. I fear that I have given the children (ages ten, six, and four) negative impressions of themselves. I have failed to be a good example and have been inadequate in dealing with the problem.
- I feel guilty and disappointed in myself—plus I usually don't get over my anger as fast as when I deal calmly with the children.

There is a major danger in permitting an ongoing sense of inadequacy to overwhelm you. Children do need correction and discipline. Don't believe for one minute that we are advocates of permissive, passive child-rearing practices! When we feel overly guilty or inadequate, then we can make a mistake in the opposite direction by being too lenient with a child after we have screamed at him or her.

Grace made this mistake one day. Grace had vowed, even as a child, that *she* would never yell at *her* children. But the time came when she broke that vow and yelled at her seven-year-old son. When she had finished, she sent him to his room to think it over.

He was not the one who did the most thinking, however. Grace suddenly saw in his remorseful young face her own childish feelings when her mother yelled. She began to consider his age and size and believed she had been unrealistic in her expectations. In fact, Grace became so remorseful and guilt-ridden that she took action.

She placed a slice of her son's favorite chocolate cake and a glass of cold milk on a tray. Bearing this offering of condolence and reparation, she went to his room where he was leaning over his desk in pensive thought. As that perceptive lad realized what his mom had for him, he said, "Mom, you just spoiled the whole thing!" He realized that he needed the correction and her offering took that away.

Guilt and over-identification with her son resulted in Grace's mistake. Screaming wasn't the answer, but rewarding the child with cake wasn't the answer either. Life is a constant search for balances in too much, too little, too soon, and too late. Admittedly it isn't easy to find that midpoint, but most of us can be better than we are. In the last chapter we will offer you some help with your struggles over guilt.

SHAME OR EMBARRASSMENT

Guilt was the mothers' number one feeling after screaming. The next reaction of moms to their own screaming was shame or embarrassment.

- Since I grew up with a screaming mother, I hate it, and I hate myself for repeating such shameful behavior. I don't believe that instilling fear is a useful form of discipline—yet that's what screaming does.
- I feel ashamed and more upset because I know my screaming only adds to the problem.
- I feel very unhappy and ashamed of myself. To make matters worse, my sixteen- and fifteen-year-olds check the calendar to see if it's close to my monthly grouch time!

If you are one of the mothers who feel such shame and remorse, count yourself fortunate. Like guilt, shame can prompt you to change. Since it is a painful emotion, we work very hard to overcome and avoid it.

When you feel embarrassed, you may very well begin to understand your children. They, too, feel embarrassed and ashamed when you yell at them. As you overcome your shame, perhaps you will be able to help your children heal from their embarrassment. Together you can grow in self-control, the genuine strength of true gentleness, and the self-respect we all need.

Obviously, to avoid the shame you will need to break your habit of screaming and replace it with new methods of training and discipline. In chapters 6 and 7, we'll give you some guidelines.

RELEASE—I FEEL BETTER

Several perceptive and honest mothers admitted to feeling better after yelling at their children. Screaming seemed to relieve their tension and frustration temporarily. Later they experienced guilt or shame.

- Usually it makes me feel better to blow off steam. But after a little while I feel guilty, and I realize that there could have been a much better way to handle the situation. I end up having to apologize to my children for my wrong behavior.

- Right after I scream I feel like justifying myself. Yes, I really did have a reason to get angry. It was the last straw. Then we go from there—we apologize, discuss, and then lay it to rest, permanently. I always hated it when my mom reminded me how bad I'd been two hours or two days or two weeks or two years ago. In my home, we aim to forget the problem and move on!

After releasing their emotions, these mothers feel calm. One child described his mom after a time of screaming as being "normal" for several days. He endured her yelling for the blessed respite from her anger, that period of calm after the storm.

While some moms are aware of the onslaught of remorse after they experience the relief, many are not so fortunate. A mother might enjoy the relief and remain unaware that she leaves her children devastated by helpless, sad, frightened, and angry feelings. She may only perceive her children as more compliant, or, because they withdraw, "out of her hair."

If you are one of these moms, please step back and take a look at yourself. We know that you *do* love your children. We suspect you simply have not recognized what your explosive lectures are doing to them. You can change. We hope you will try!

A Sense of Power

When some mothers scream, they receive a sense of power. In chapter 2 we described why mothers scream. One of the reasons was the sense of powerlessness many mothers experience. When Susan was asked how she felt after screaming, she replied that she discovered "a sense of power that comes with anger." Obviously it *is* anger that prompts yelling. Melissa agreed with Susan:

After feeling so completely frustrated, screaming restores the sense of power to me, makes me feel that I really am in charge of the situation. Of course, this feeling passes rapidly, and I am back to feeling helpless.

It seems that the answer to this set of mothers' responses is the acquisition of true strength. Since they use angry screaming to work up a sense of power, it is apparent that they feel helpless and are trying desperately to bolster their areas of weakness.

They must realize that everyone is given some assets. We only have to recognize them, choose to develop them, and use them. But it is fear and inexperience that defeat us, and usually these grow out of the helpless years of our childhood. Learn to recognize your needs and feelings. Name and discuss them until you catch them *before* you resort to the deceptive power of screaming to cover them.

For example, if you feel weak and uncertain, why not admit it? Your child no doubt senses that anyway and will respect you more, not less, for admitting your anxiety. Say something like this: "Sally, when you fail to stop watching television to do your jobs and schoolwork, I feel worried and sad. Because I do so much for you, I'd like you to show me your appreciation by helping me. I worry about your future when you seem to care so little about learning and being responsible." Having spoken honestly about your own feelings, you might ask Sally how she feels and if she'd like to see some changes. Try to involve her in solutions to *your* concerns about *her* problems that can eliminate your screaming.

Whether you feel guilty, ashamed, powerful, "better," or a mix of these emotions, you need to pay attention to your feelings. Understanding how screaming makes you feel is one of the keys to finding a way to stop.

■ ■ ■

CHAPTER 5

MISSION IMPOSSIBLE?

"Please help me. I don't want to scream, really I don't. Each time it happens, I tell myself that I'll work harder to change, that it won't happen again, and yet it always does. Why do I keep doing what I hate?"

According to our experience and investigation, all children and most mothers hate screaming. We have just discussed the many profoundly negative feelings that result from screaming episodes. Guilt, sadness, shame, anger, and a desire to hide or run away are only a few of the painful reactions to screaming. So why do mothers continue to yell? What makes it so difficult to stop?

HABIT

When habits become ingrained in a person's lifestyle, they become extremely hard to break. When those habits have extended through generations of a family, the patterns become even more difficult to change.

> When I think of my mother, I see her screaming at my brother
> or me over something trivial and always—always—making big
> issues out of inconsequentials. My mother felt the same way
> about my grandmother, and now my children tell me that I
> overreact and continually make a big deal over nothing!

But there is hope. Any habit can be broken. No matter what the underlying reason for those habits may be (and we will discuss those next), you can break them. Of course, first you must want to. But more importantly you must *decide* to. You will need a specific plan not only to stop your yelling but also to substitute a more successful, new habit. In chapter 6, we will outline a simple plan for you to use. For now let's look at what makes it so hard for moms to stop screaming.

LACK OF KNOWLEDGE ABOUT ALTERNATIVES

Because of family patterns, most of us parent our children in one of two ways—*like* our parents or *opposite* from them. Both extremes may be equally erroneous. A woman who grows up with a screaming mother may find it harder to stop than if she had grown up without the screaming. Another woman will vow never to scream but may over-react by becoming too passive and end up being thought of as a "wimp" by her children. However, it is possible to develop a balanced parenting style.

There are four sources for learning about new and different parenting skills. *Television,* if viewed thoughtfully, can teach both positive and negative modes of parenting. *Books* and *articles* can give excellent ideas on good discipline and training skills. Likewise, the Internet offers many articles online. *Other parents* (good or bad) can provide a rich source of different techniques in handling children. *Your own parental instincts* can guide you in many situations. Be careful, however, to differentiate between the God-given quality of instinctive parenting and your own impulsiveness.

Children themselves also offer some wise alternatives to screaming. While we may not agree to allowing children to place their responsibilities second to television viewing, there is some wisdom in these suggestions from children. Listen to Laurie's story:

> My mom usually screams at me when I am supposed to be
> cleaning the hamster cage but I am playing something or

watching television. Then she says, "GET OVER HERE!" and she starts screaming at me, and I start talking back to her and we get in a big fight, and she usually wins and I get grounded. I think that my mom could have let me clean the hamster cage when the television program was over.

How often mothers scream because they are overwhelmed with fatigue and heavy responsibilities! Elizabeth, a fourth grader, makes a suggestion that's right on target.

One Tuesday after school I was watching television. When my mom came home she was in a real bad mood. She walked in the door and turned off the television. Then she took the madness out on me by screaming at me. I felt really bad for the rest of the day. I think my mom could have taken a nap to get around screaming. There is always a way to get around screaming.

LACK OF SELF-CONTROL

Mothers also find it is a struggle to stop screaming because they have not been taught adequate self-control. Interestingly, it is often in an attempt to teach self-control to children that mothers lose their own control. Recently I received a letter from a mother (much like the mother we discussed earlier) who was desperate about her two-year-old's toilet training. She would sit with him for a long time while he was on his potty with no results—only to have him immediately make a mess in his clean diaper when she let him off the potty. Once she "lost it" and, to her horror, began screaming at him and shaking him. Many mothers lose control over problems that are even less distressing than dirty diapers during potty training.

Self-control begins as the product of good, external controls exerted by parents on young children. The first three years are by far the most important era of life. During those first crucial months, children learn to control their physical functions—to sit, crawl, and walk. Then they learn to eat, and they finally gain bowel and bladder control.

At two, toddlers learn to say no to almost every request of their parents. Soon they learn to bend their wills and adapt to the demands of family living. The temper tantrums common to almost all toddlers have much to do with their needs to test adult controls and to pit their wills and wishes against their parents. It is extremely important for parents to exert healthy authority over a child if he or she is to learn self-control. The best control possible, by the way, is that of lovingly but very securely holding that child until the tantrum is over. It is exactly such loving, tangible, external control that first enables a young child to begin to exert self-control.

The next stage of self-control is acquiring a sense of responsibility. By kindergarten age, children must learn to take turns, share, and cooperate with others. They must assume major responsibilities for themselves, such as doing schoolwork and performing a number of tasks around the home. All of these jobs demand a great deal of self-control.

During adolescence control extends to social behaviors and is extremely important in handling sexual feelings and desires. The need to collaborate in team sports, in school groups, and on part-time jobs requires great self-control.

Those who reach adult life without mastering the skill of self-control are likely to find themselves in all sorts of difficulty. Certainly they are at risk to be screaming parents. To develop self-control as an adult on your own is a heroic task. Nevertheless, it *is* possible, and we urge you to work at it. Chapter 6 will give specific steps to help you master this skill.

If you have not yet learned self-control you will struggle to teach it to your children. But your teaching will have tremendously positive effects later on.

LACK OF MOTIVATION

Other mothers who feel they should stop screaming but struggle to do so are often plagued by a lack of motivation. Several mothers told us they believed that screaming worked. Why? Because their children would finally obey them when they yelled. Others felt powerful, as if they had finally gained control over their children. So why should they change?

Of course, we can give a very good reason—the cost of screaming's apparent success is just too high. All mothers are familiar with determining whether a cost is reasonable. Maybe the dazzling new outfit you'd love to have simply won't fit your budget. The luxury of convenience foods is tempting, but you know the total bill would horrify you at the grocery checkout counter.

That's the way it is with screaming. It *seems* powerful and successful, but the price includes resentment, fear, and a silent vow for revenge in your child. As soon as he or she is bigger or feels more powerful than you, there will be a showdown—and no one will win.

Jane remembers the day she grabbed her mother's arms when her mother started screaming at her and slapping her. She realized on that day that she was stronger than her mother. And on that day her mother's influence over Jane's life virtually ended.

So think carefully and with a long-range perspective. If you do, we believe you will become motivated to change your habit of screaming.

FAILURE TO UNDERSTAND THE POWER TO CHOOSE

Some parents continue screaming because they don't realize they have a choice. As a psychiatrist, Grace has become impressed with the many people who do not realize that they can *choose* not only how they will act and react, but how they will feel as well. One patient told her that the most important fact he had learned in forty-five years of life is that very one: "I can choose!" The gift of choice was given to people by the Creator, but many of us not only fail to recognize it, we fail to use it and therefore miss the benefit.

We have so little control over many things that happen to us, but we do have ultimate control over how we will respond to those happenings around us. When a child breaks our favorite vase or tears a precious book while we are on the telephone, we can decide: Will we rage at the child in frustration? Or will we calmly and firmly teach that parts of the house and special items demand different behaviors? "You do not throw a ball near the shelf where pretty things are arranged!" Or, "You do not treat books carelessly!" We may even need to exercise the choice of putting certain items out of reach of our children until they learn to be careful.

To master the art of choosing how you will respond instead of blindly reacting, try these steps:

1. Identify clearly whatever feeling you are experiencing.
2. Determine why you feel that way.
3. Decide what you will do to correct the problem and erase the emotion.
4. Follow through with the action.

There is always something we can do about any situation. Sometimes it is only our own attitudes and responses over which we have control. If so, then exercise that in the most positive, constructive way possible.

Choosing how you respond does not mean that you become so "patient" that you end up being permissive. It only means that you will react firmly, clearly, and fairly so your children will benefit from your healthy authority.

Ricky said he felt "bad for the thing I did wrong, but she [Mom] doesn't have to scream. She can say, 'Please don't watch television.'" He is right; she *can* say that firmly without yelling.

BASICALLY ANGRY PEOPLE

If you spend some time observing people's faces, you can learn to read their dominant emotions. Airports are great places for this! If you watch closely enough, you are likely to observe many facial expressions. Some people look angry even when they seem to be relaxed. Their eyes focus intently, their jaws are set in hard lines, and their lips look tightly pressed.

Such angry people will have trouble controlling their screaming. They may have learned to cover their hurts and fears with a protective coat of armor—aggression. They think the shield will deflect any more hurt from their lives. And in some ways, the shield works. But unfortunately, it makes them unaware of their harshness, of the way in which they hurt others—especially their children.

Angry mothers often yell without even realizing it. And this combination of an angry face and a screaming voice can overwhelm a sensitive child.

Angry moms are often insensitive to the child's painful feelings. Such a lack is not due to a mother's badness, but it is a part of the emotional hardness that has helped her survive the tough times she has had to endure. These calluses may protect the mother, but they prevent her sensitivity to the children she actually loves very much!

Correcting such a problem is no easy task. Begin with admitting to yourself that you have become angry. Look honestly at your face in a mirror. Do you see the telltale expression of anger there? Ask a loving and honest friend. Does she see you as an aggressive, easily angered woman?

If what you see and hear reflect to you a basic anger, begin breaking those habits. The blueprints for remodeling an angry, bitter personality into one of love and clear thinking are waiting for you! And they are definitely worth your time and attention.

■ ■ ■

CHAPTER 6

How to Get Control

of Yourself

As the biblical book of Proverbs tells us, that woman who is cool and collected, who is master of her countenance, her voice, her actions, and her gestures, will be the mother who is in control of her children, and who is greatly beloved by them (chapter 31).

Like it or not, mothers set the tone of the home. As a mother, you have probably noticed that when you are in control, the children are much easier to keep under control. But when you are upset for any reason, the children are usually "off the wall." Children are sensitive; they respond dramatically to the emotional pulse of the mother.

We've already discussed what causes mothers to lose control. Now let's look at some positive ways to gain control.

PLANNING AND ORGANIZATION

A controlled mother plans ahead and is organized. Remember—you need to be the *master* of the day rather than the *victim.* It is vital to have a strategy for the day that includes anticipating potential problems and planning how to deal with them.

Problems arise when most of life is a surprise and you are caught off guard and unprepared. When this happens, you can automatically be thrown out of control until you regroup and sort out the chaos of the moment.

Rita, a newly organized mother, tells this story:

I used to just get up and let the day happen. It happened all right,
and most of it was bad. Everyone else was controlling my life—
my children, my husband, my friends. I began to feel used,
abused, and resentful, and decided to make a change. I wanted to
feel that I had some control, even a little, over my life and time.

To help myself get organized, I began to make lists on little
scraps of paper that I would misplace and lose. Oh well! I felt I
was on the right track. Later on, I bought an organizer, and
actually began to enjoy writing down my plans for the day, the
week, the month. It became a game to see how many of the
things I had written down I could actually get done.

Little by little, my family and friends began to have some
respect for my time and my plans. I really feel it has been
because I can say I am doing certain other things, and, wonder
of wonders, I am even learning to say no to foolish requests.

For many people, becoming organized is far from easy—it is heroic.
Kim wanted very much to keep a neat house, get the laundry done in
a timely fashion, prepare nourishing meals, and spend time with her
children. But for years she zigzagged. When the house was clean the
laundry piled up, and when the meals were outstanding she had a
messy house.

One day, in desperation, she viewed the small mountain of laundry, her messy house, and her quarrelsome children. She decided to
take charge of her home and family. First she made a list, carefully
arranging the jobs to be done. She packed the dirty laundry in six
heavy-duty trash bags and took them to her local laundry. While it
washed and dried she read to her children and then got them to help
fold and carefully put away their own things.

Next she put a tasty but simple dinner in the oven. While it
cooked, she and her husband and the children raced through the house

picking up and putting things away. Soon the house was in order, the laundry heap had vanished, and a delicious and attractive meal graced the table. Her husband and children were proud and amazed to have been a part of the transformation. But best of all, she knew she could manage the demands of her household—because she had learned how to plan, prioritize, and follow through. So can you.

FLEXIBILITY

While planning ahead, a controlled mother is also flexible. Some moms tend to make following a schedule more important than meeting the needs of their children. This rigidity will result in loss of control and, ultimately, in screaming. Life is full of interruptions, emergencies, crises, and urgent happenings. A mother must train herself to go with the flow, even if it means temporarily abandoning her plan or realizing that it goes against the natural inclinations of her personality. It isn't always easy, especially at the start, but the rewards are tremendous.

Although Kate struggled with flexibility for months, she found it reaped great benefits in her family life.

> When my daughter was a toddler, she reached that stage where she wanted to touch everything. She knew what no meant, and she heard it often!
>
> I had great plans for one particular Saturday and needed to leave the house, but my daughter was exerting her very strong will. She reached out to touch something. I said no but she touched it anyway. I pushed her hand away to reaffirm that it was no! This did not deter her, and she touched the object again and again.
>
> I was irritated and perplexed. Should I stay at home and deal with this behavior pattern she was exhibiting, or should I carry on with my plans? I really felt we were at a crisis point, and that she needed moment by moment consistency. I reluctantly

cancelled my plans and stayed home, spending much of the day saying no.

I'm so glad I did. Although she was much harder to train in that area than my other children, the block of time spent in training her paid off. She learned that no meant no and that she needed to respect property and not touch everything in sight.

While mothers often need to be flexible in terms of changing their own plans, there is another type of flexibility that will help prevent screaming: Know when to bend the rules and give just a bit. Although children require consistency, they also need to have special privileges now and then. Knowing when to allow a shorter practice time or a bit longer television time can create a bond of appreciation that will strengthen your love. Your children will realize that you extend consideration to them.

If your child has had an especially tough day at school, is pestered by a brother or sister, and has a load of homework, it may be extremely useful to allow him to skip practicing piano or doing dishes for one night. Be careful, though, to make such exceptions a rarity so the child will not learn to manipulate but rather to accept the gesture as a gift.

A SENSE OF HUMOR

A controlled mother has a sense of humor. The mother who can laugh at herself, with the children, and at the impossible situations of life rather than take them too seriously is far ahead on the road to personal control. Having the wisdom to step back and see the humor of her situation helped Sharon gain control:

> It was the night of the school Christmas pageant and the first program the older two had ever been in. At that time, I had a four-year-old girl, a three-year-old girl, and a baby of nine months. My husband was gone, and the children were constantly at each other.

Besides that, so many little things went wrong. Socks to wear with dresses were missing, the children had each spilled food all over themselves and their clothes, hair was extra unruly, and I was exhausted with the ordeal of getting them ready and out the door. When I discovered the car keys were missing, I felt frustration plus! Believe me, I was literally ready to tear my hair out.

Suddenly I realized how funny the whole situation was! I was in the middle of a situation comedy that no one would ever see but me! I sat down in the middle of the floor and began to laugh. I laughed so hard the tears came. My children didn't know what to think at first. They sat down on the floor with me and put their arms around me. But you know what? We found the keys—under a pillow, of all places—and just barely managed to get to the program in time.

BALANCE

A controlled mother strives to keep balance in her life. A mother is often frustrated and weary at the end of the day—not only because of her workload but also because she has not had time to pursue activities that are important to her personal growth and development. Since stimulation dispels boredom and fatigue, change can give fulfillment to the inner being while releasing frustration and increasing enthusiasm.

You may feel as if each day becomes a juggling act. You have to balance commitment to your husband, your children, your home, and your work, and yet have some time to pursue special projects, compelling interests, and friendships. Whew! What a task! But achieving balance can change your attitude toward your children. It did for Carol.

I almost went crazy being a mother. I had three children in five years and was under a daily load of laundry, dishes, a house strewn with paraphernalia, and sticky fingerprints decorating my walls. I had been an art designer and longed to spend time alone in what had once been my studio but was now a catch-all room! I was so frustrated with never having time for my art that I began to wish I'd never had children. Then I would feel guilty and miserable.

For a while I assumed I was the only mother who had ever felt trapped. Then I confided my feelings to another mother of three. She felt the same way. We thought of a plan to baby-sit twice a week for each other for a half day. We've been doing it now for almost a year. Having that time alone to pursue my artwork has made all the difference to me and to my children. I can now enjoy them, knowing I'll have some well-earned time for myself.

Other helpful suggestions for finding your balance in life may occur to you. We suggest learning to say no to tasks you may be asked (and even wish) to do. When your children are more independent, you can consider taking on additional jobs.

We sometimes wonder why mothers don't think about hiring a baby-sitter when they are at home. An older child may love to baby-sit while you do something you'd like or even take a nap! It costs very little, helps a young person earn a little money and experience, and offers a fresh opportunity for your children to expand their relationships.

Finally, learning that deep cleaning and some other household tasks can wait for a time (even several years!) can relieve your mind. If you are an orderly person, it may be just as hard for you to let certain jobs go undone as it is for the disorganized mothers to learn to plan and prioritize. But try it. It could help you find your balance.

A Positive Attitude

A controlled mother has a positive attitude. The psychologist William James said, "The greatest discovery of my generation is that you can change your circumstances by changing your attitudes of mind." Here is a classic illustration of a mother with a positive attitude:

> Great-great-grandmother, on a winter's day,
> milked the cows and fed them hay,
> slopped the hogs, saddled the mule,
> then got the children off to school,
> did a washing, mopped the floors,
> washed the windows, and did some chores;
> cooked a dish of home-dried fruit,
> pressed her husband's Sunday suit.
> Swept the parlor, made the bed,
> baked a dozen loaves of bread,
> split some firewood, and then lugged in
> enough to fill the kitchen bin;
> cleaned the lamps and put in oil,
> stewed some apples she thought would spoil;
> churned the butter, baked a cake,
> then exclaimed, "For heaven's sake,
> the calves have got out of the pen"—
> went out and chased them in again.
>
> Gathered the eggs and locked the stable,
> back to the house and set the table,
> cooked a supper that was delicious,
> and afterward washed up all the dishes,
> fed the cat and sprinkled the clothes,
> mended a basketful of hose;
> then opened the organ and began to play,
> "When You Come to the End of a Perfect Day."
>   —Author Unknown

This great lady was in control of herself and her life largely because of an incredibly positive attitude toward her responsibilities.

If you happen to be a more critical person, you may find it difficult to change your attitude. Don't expect an immediate transformation—just try to add some hopeful comments in the midst of any criticism you feel you need to state. Solving problems together, correcting mistakes with kindness, and forgiving each other can restore hope to your child and strengthen the love between you.

It is not easy to plan ahead, to be flexible, to have a sense of humor when frustrated, to keep a balanced life, and to have a positive attitude. But each is a worthy and attainable goal for the mother who longs to stop screaming and get control of herself. Each is possible to attain most of the time if you have the courage to replace screaming with organization, flexibility, humor, balance, and a positive attitude.

Ralph Waldo Emerson wrote, "That which we persist in doing becomes easier for us to do; not that the nature of the thing itself is changed, but that our power to do is increased."

A PRESCRIPTION FOR CHANGE

A controlled mother has a prescription for change. You mothers who scream realize, of course, that you do it for a good reason. We have reviewed many of those causes in chapter 2 and why it's so hard to stop in chapter 5. Now we'd like to offer you some clear and proven steps that will enable you to change.

Find the Motivation

Breaking any habit is so much trouble that one must truly want to do it. Few habits are harder to break than screaming. Some images that may motivate you are

- happier, better adjusted children;

- a day filled with good feelings rather than the shame or remorse you experience after yelling;
- the approval of your spouse, parents, or friends of your new behaviors;
- the confidence that comes when you learn better, more successful parenting skills.

If these images are not enough to help you change, then perhaps you need another motivator. Try leaving on a tape recorder during a stressful time that usually prompts screaming. Then listen to yourself. How do you sound when you scream at your children? Is that how you want them to remember you?

Every time you are tempted to scream, remember how you sound when you do. It may give you the motivation you need to stop.

Give Yourself Permission to Change

This idea may sound foolish at first, but think about it. Chances are you yell because you were taught to yell—by your mother, by accidentally discovering it worked, or by some other means. To begin to change, then, you must believe it's okay not to yell and that you can find better methods.

It's good to discuss with someone else your ideas for changing. A person who has found ways of handling children without screaming is one of your best allies.

Decide Firmly to Change

How often we think about breaking a habit. Do these thoughts sound familiar? *I* ought *to go on a diet!* Or, *I really* should *learn to control my spending.* And, *I* need *to organize my time better.* All of these words *(ought, should,* and *need)* are emphatic and indicate intentions to change. But that change will not happen automatically.

We recommend that you think, clearly and emphatically, something like this: *I know my screaming does more damage than good. I* choose *to stop screaming, and I will begin to break that habit today.* It takes a definite decision and commitment to effect change.

Formulate a Plan

Outline a goal that is *possible* for you to reach. Each day, can you scream one time less than the day before? On at least one occasion when you would normally yell, make yourself avoid doing so. Learn to recognize the early warning signs of an emotional storm. Before that storm bursts, put your feelings into words: "I feel *anxious* that I may be unable to handle this problem." Or, "I am just *furious* because you misused my computer!!" Thinking about your emotions will begin to put you in control of them—instead of allowing them to take control of you.

Next, think about what really has upset you so much. On the surface, of course, it's something your child has said or done—or *not* done! But when you consider a situation a bit more, you will often discover some underlying memory or a deep fear of losing parental authority. We have even known mothers whose children acted very much like their grandparents. One mother faintly heard her father's domineering voice in her daughter's bossy back talk.

Knowing how you feel and why you feel that way will enable you to make a pivotal decision. "What will I do about this situation that will really cure it?" You may take time out in order to plan the answer carefully. Waiting for your action is a very useful part of the disciplinary response children need. (Later we'll share an example of the power of silence.) They can ponder their misbehavior and become a bit anxious. Being uncomfortable inside may help them decide to overcome problem habits!

Find Some Help

To change any habit, we need a friend to remind us when we fall into the old patterns and to encourage us when the going gets rough. Find that special person and ask her if she will be available to you for several weeks. When you are about to resort to screaming, run to the phone and call for help. If you fail to reach your goals for a day or more, tell her you need encouragement. Even if the friend you need desperately is not there when you call, the act of trying can give you the time to regain your control.

And don't forget that God is always on call. Contact him for the patience and wisdom you will need. One way to communicate with him is to imagine his presence near you. After you ask for help, listen! You may be amazed, not at hearing a physical voice, but at the unique ideas that pop into your mind.

Follow Through

The best plans in the world will fall flat unless you put them to work. People often say, "I really tried that idea, but it didn't work." With some mental exploring, they often discover that they unwittingly expected it to work just by talking about it. *You* must work the plan day after day, even when it seems unsuccessful. Bad habits take time to develop, and changes also take time. You may never know how close to success you were because you gave up just short of the finish line. It's at such a point of discouragement that your friend can be of the most value.

Professional Help

As we have already said, there are some reasons for screaming that have a physical basis. Be sure to see your doctor on a regular basis and keep your body healthy.

Equally common are some psychological, emotional, and even spiritual "blind spots" that may prevent your seeing issues clearly. You may have convinced yourself that screaming is okay since it seems to work. Possibly you are unable to see how it is angering or scaring your child.

We urge you to have a personal and a family checkup. A good family counselor can see issues more clearly and objectively than you, who are so close to them. That counsel can be invaluable. Often only a few visits can get you past the pressure points to a place where you can develop and carry out new methods of discipline *and* build a loving relationship at the same time.

We know you can do it!

Chapter 7

Corralling Your Kids

Happy, smiling faces. Busy fingers, helping hands. The music of their laughter. The dancing of their feet. Good times together without tiresome whining or ugly pouting. All who look nod and smile…the beauty of the well behaved.

Every mother's dream is to speak softly and get a cheerful, obedient response from attentive, cooperative children. *An impossible dream?* No, but it requires that the mother behave as the controlled, firm, loving, fair, consistent authority figure who *chooses* not to scream. There is a way to make this dream become your reality.

Velvet over steel is a three-word picture of the mother who is fun, loving, soft, and gentle, yet exudes strength and control. The undergirding of strength and control allows her to be fun-loving with her children and even permits her to act silly. She can do it because she is still in control of herself and in control of her children. She knows it, and they know it!

Steel gives strength and meaning to each word the mother speaks. Steel doesn't need to scream, "I am strong. Please believe me, I really am strong!" Steel *is* strong. Steel can be a raised eyebrow, a look on a mother's face, a glance across a room, or a meeting of eyes that penetrates the heart of an understanding child.

Velvet is what every mother wants to be, the part of the mother's personality she wants to reveal. The undergirding of steel makes it possible.

The velvet-over-steel mother controls her children in three very positive ways. Let's discuss them.

SAY WHAT YOU MEAN, AND
MEAN WHAT YOU SAY

The velvet-over-steel mother says what she means and means what she says—all of the time. This requires thinking, planning, and following through with confidence, and, above all, consistency. A mother must learn to be consistent, even when she is tired, overcommitted, and under excessive stress. A mother can choose to discipline herself to be consistent regardless of what is going on (or not going on) in her life. Consistency with the children will reap rewards that will help the rest of life to fall into proper perspective.

When you sense the breaking point coming, rather than screaming, take time to be silent and think. Think about the consequences of what you are going to say and do so you can be a mother without regrets.

Grocery stores are an inevitable problem for mothers of young children. This mother unfortunately said something she really did not mean:

> I was busy, running late, had to fix dinner, and had an evening
> class to attend. Time was of the essence. My five-year-old was
> cranky and uncooperative. I asked him to get a box of cereal for
> himself. He loudly snapped, "No, I won't." Other shoppers
> heard his overly loud remark as they wheeled their carts by. I
> knew I had to do something, but what? If I spanked him, he
> would just get louder. I felt myself getting more angry as well as
> embarrassed. Out of sheer frustration, I screamed, "I'm NEVER
> bringing you here again!"

How fortunate for this five-year-old! He never wanted to go to the boring grocery store in the first place. But what will the mother do? Has she really disciplined her son, or has she punished herself? For the next few years, is she really going to the grocery store only when her son is in school or when she has someone else to watch him? She has trapped herself in a very difficult situation by not taking the time to assess her options and the consequences for both herself and her son before taking action.

While she is thinking and planning what course of action to take, a mother's silence can be momentarily misunderstood by the child and interpreted as his or her getting away with the unacceptable behavior. But in time the child will learn to have a healthy respect for Mother's silence.

For example, several years ago, Pat entered the house with her fifth-grade daughter, was going through the mail, and became unusually silent. Her eighth-grade son's grades had come and were not in keeping with his ability, nor were they at the level of previous years. She was thinking about how to handle the situation before approaching him.

Her daughter sensed the unnatural silence and asked, "Mom, have I done anything wrong?"

Pat responded, "No, why do you ask?"

"Well," her daughter said, "you are being very, very quiet, and you have that real serious look on your face—the one you get when one of us has done something."

Pat immediately reassured her daughter, and for the first time began to be consciously aware not only of the wisdom of silence in discipline but also of the power of silence in discipline.

Practicing the art of silence is one of the most difficult disciplines in this world, at least for many of us! That is why we have written about learning and using self-control. If you will master this skill and use it to stay quiet instead of impulsively screaming out your rage and demands, you may transform your family life. Once you have conquered the screaming habit, replace it with self-control, silence, and thoughtfulness. Then you will know what you mean to say, and you can say what you really mean.

Probably the most important benefit to a mother who means what she says and says what she means is that her child is given a firm foundation of trust and confidence. The child knows that he or she can count on what the mother says because she means it. The child doesn't need to argue and whine because the mother means what she says the first time. Arguing and whining are largely eliminated when the mother is confident that her decisions are fair and right. She cannot be worn down or manipulated because she is secure, and the child can trust her. She means every word she says, whether it is a treat promised or a disciplinary action. The mother will not forget or change her mind when she cools down or when other things interfere. Because his world is predictable, the child feels secure and gains self-esteem. Remember that predictability is one of the most vital emotional needs of every child.

State the Desired Behavior and Results Ahead of Time

A mother needs to state the desired behavior ahead of time and what the positive and negative consequences will be. The mother who sets limits ahead of time, explains what is expected, what the reward for obedience will be, and what the result of disobedience will be, can never be labeled as unfair. Why? The choice to obey or disobey becomes the choice of the child. For example, let's take another look at the grocery store scene. This mother had explained to her child that good behavior in the store meant he could pick out something for himself at the end of the trip—a treat of some sort. Misbehavior meant he missed out on the treat and might lose a privilege when he got home. Here's what happened:

> I was busy, running late, had to fix dinner, and had an evening class to attend. Time was of the essence. My five-year-old was cranky and uncooperative. I asked him to get a box of cereal for himself. He loudly snapped, "No, I won't."

The mother looked seriously and sternly at her son and said in a soft but firm voice, "You know what to do in this grocery store. We went over what to do, and you told me all the right things. You need to do them each and every time we are here. Because you chose not to do the right things and help me, you will not get a treat from the store and you will not be able to go to Jimmy's house to play ball when we get home."

The little boy began to sniffle, and Mom responded, "I'm very sorry that you did not choose to obey, and I hope that this will help you to remember how to help Mommy the next time we come to the store."

Unlike the mother in the first sequence, this mother knows that there will be many, many grocery-store trips with her son. He simply must learn to cooperate or suffer the consequences. In the past, she has reviewed the grocery-store standards of behavior and made it clear to him that there will be consequences if he misbehaves. He may lose out on the positive reward of a grocery-store treat that he was to enjoy for being helpful during a rather boring time for him and he may miss playing when he gets home. This loss of privilege will help him to remember to behave the next time he goes to the grocery store with his mother.

This loving mother has set a behavioral standard of grocery-store cooperation, and she feels it is wise and correct. The boy knew what was expected ahead of time and had verbalized the behavior so that the mother was certain he understood. The boy chose to misbehave. The mother did not respond from anger or embarrassment but simply followed through with a previously arranged agreement.

Stating the desired behavior ahead of time, and what the positive and negative consequences will be, works with teenagers as well. Let's continue the story of Pat's son's grades.

I was stunned at his first quarter eighth-grade marks. He had always been an excellent student. Frankly, there had never been a need to discuss consequences of poor grades until this time. I first told my son I wanted to talk with him after dinner. (I don't believe that mealtime should be destroyed with unpleasant conversation, and the matter didn't involve his sister, anyway.) He said, "Sure," but wondered why. I told him to be prepared to discuss his report card, knowing that waiting for discipline can enhance its effectiveness by allowing the child to think about the issue.

After dinner I showed him the grades and asked for his explanation. He told me he hadn't studied as he should have, had missed turning in some assignments, and had generally not applied himself. I asked what he planned to do in the next quarter. He told me that he would study harder, turn in assignments, and apply himself.

All that sounded good, but being a firm believer in positive and negative consequences, I needed to do more. I asked him if he liked attending the private school he was at. He did. I asked him if he wanted to continue there. He did. I told him that if his grades improved, his father and I would continue paying the tuition that enabled him to attend this private school (the positive consequence) but that if his grades did not improve, then he would forfeit the right to attend the school and would be placed elsewhere (the negative consequence).

My son knew I meant what I said and that the choice was his—to do better and remain in the school or save his parents a lot of expense and be placed elsewhere. His grades improved steadily; he stayed in the school, graduated with honors, and we never had such a talk regarding grades again.

Balancing positive and negative consequences is a continual challenge for the mother because what is positive and negative for a child varies from age to age and stage to stage. A mother must know what is important to the child and will often be surprised by how simple the positive really can be.

Tammy, the mother of a second grader, was having a struggle getting her little girl to assume simple responsibilities around the house. She had "tried everything" and "nothing worked." We spoke casually with the little girl and found out that "the best thing of all is going to the doughnut shop on Saturday mornings!" Her mother had never realized that this meant so much to the little girl. Encouraging the child with a visit to the doughnut shop was just the motivation the little girl needed to complete her chores.

As children grow in their ability to understand a reason, include them in establishing rules for family living. They are often helpful in deciding on the positive and negative consequences as well. After all, who should know better than the child what will be most meaningful to him or her in learning important lessons?

One family set up a weekly family council. In a friendly, businesslike fashion, they discussed all the concerns of each family member—what they needed, special privileges that required certain activities, who had a quarrel against whom, and whose household jobs were especially well done (or needed more attention). Their communications system worked so well they discovered that no one needed to scream anymore. Eventually this family used their council time to express their appreciation and respect and just to have fun together.

MAKE A CONSCIOUS CHOICE TO ENJOY YOUR CHILDREN

The velvet-over-steel mother makes a conscious choice to *enjoy* her children. Since the child-rearing path is strewn with so many hazards, mothers need to determine to enjoy their children rather than to grimly accept the current stage (the "I can't wait till it's over" syndrome).

A very wise mother of eight once said, "Your child has the right to be the age he or she is for 365 days, just as you have the right to be the age you are for 365 days." Accepting this as fair, mothers might just as well decide to pass the year in enjoyment rather than with seething frustration that erupts with frequent bouts of screaming.

Making this philosophy work demands that you learn something about the capabilities of children at a particular age. Read books or articles on child development. Observe the children of relatives and friends, and talk with those parents. Watch your own child, and see what she is able to do by herself. Remember, each child is unique, so no two will have identical capacities, but you can collect some guidelines that will enable you to be more fair.

This little motto has helped Grace discover how to enjoy her children: Explore—before you expect! As you encourage, observe, listen, and teach, you will not only enjoy, but, we believe, become excited as you watch your children develop!

In an ancient Chinese alphabet, the characters used to describe *crisis* are interpreted in English as "dangerous opportunity." That is exactly what every disciplinary situation is—a dangerous opportunity. *If* the mother exercises self-control and chooses to be fair, firm, loving, and consistent, the crisis situation becomes an exciting opportunity to build character and self-esteem in her children and to enhance her loving relationship with her children built on mutual love and respect. *If,* however, the mother does not exercise self-control but indulges in screaming, then she faces the dangers of reaping the harvest we have discussed.

A mother can do several specific things to increase her enjoyment of her children:

1. *Listen* to your children—really listen to their stories and ask questions that show interest, rather than questions that are critical or skeptical. Enjoy their stories; don't just tolerate them. Look at them as they talk, and stop whatever you are doing so they know you are interested.

2. *Spend time* with your children doing the things that are important to them at their age and stage. If you ask with genuine caring, they will be glad to tell you and share themselves with you. No other task is as important as this. Children *can't* wait!

3. *Talk* with them as very important persons, rather than as people who never remember to pick up clothes or take out the garbage. Try saying, "You are a neat person, and I doubt you can feel very good when you let yourself get by with a careless job!"

4. *Laugh* with them. Children are wonderful. The freshness of their stories, their creativity, and their honesty (although appalling at times!) cannot fail to make a mother laugh rather than grit her teeth or clench her jaws—*if* she chooses laughter. Laugh *with* them, and be cautious to avoid seeming to laugh *at* them.

As part of a research project several years ago, we asked approximately fifty junior-high girls, "What will you do when you are a mother?" They were encouraged to be honest and not put their names on their papers. There was no discussion of the question. Their answers reveal the importance of listening, talking, laughing, and spending time together:

- I won't scream at my children. I will have talks with them and explain why it isn't right to do bad things. If they don't learn by these talks, I will discipline them. I will tell them I love them. If they have problems at school or with friends, I will ask them if they want to talk about it. If they don't want to talk about their problems, I will tell them I care about them and their problems. Then I will sit and talk with them and try to help them with their problems.

- I think when I'm a mother, I will discipline my children enough so they won't be spoiled, but not a lot so they will hate me. We'll go together to parks and to ice cream parlors and things like that. I'll live in a cozy house, and once in a while, especially when it's raining, have a fire and pop popcorn. I think when I'm a mother, I'm going to laugh and have fun with my children.

For this moment in time, you are the mother. You are the one who is building the museum of memories. Mothers make mistakes, and that's okay. If children feel loved and supported in an atmosphere of enjoyment, they will forgive, accept, and enjoy mothers to the same degree that mothers forgive, accept, and enjoy them. Then their memories will be pleasant, and so will yours.

Grace reminisces:

> It was on a vacation that I discovered that I could enjoy my children. My husband and I were frankly a bit bored. In fact, he had fallen asleep on a sunny afternoon in our hotel room. Accidentally, I focused on the faint but merry laughter pealing from the next room. It was our children! No boredom in their room. As quietly as possible, I slipped into their room and joined their fun. Their comments and insights were hilariously funny. I felt really favored when they allowed me to laugh with them and especially important when they laughed at my efforts to be humorous. That event became a landmark in my relationship with my children. By rediscovering the enjoyment of joking and laughing together, we became a team—not opposing forces.

DEVELOP A CEREMONY FOR CHANGE

Jill had scolded and yelled at her son, Dan, for years. She was anxiety-ridden over his habit of daydreaming and procrastinating. He was late to meals, often forgot to care for his pets, and seemed unaware of time deadlines.

One day an article she read made Jill's mothering take a brand-new course. She suddenly understood that her nagging and screaming had been pushing her son away. He loved her but could not bear her disapproving lectures and angry looks. The more she yelled, the further he withdrew. There was real danger of out-and-out rebellion. Furthermore, in her concern over Dan's few (but irritating!) problems, Jill had long since forgotten to compliment Dan on his sense of humor, his kindness and generosity to others, and his basic good judgment.

After considerable thought, Jill found a convenient time to talk privately with Dan. For the first time he could recall in his thirteen years, she solemnly admitted she had been wrong. She listed all the specifics of her mistakes and clearly apologized for the hurts they had inflicted on his developing personality.

Dan hastily tried to reassure his mother. He reminded her that she was right about his procrastinating and that he needed her reminders. Jill, however, held fast. She was tempted to accept his excuses for her, but she knew too well that she had been disastrously wrong in her methods. She thanked him for his characteristic comfort but held to her apology.

Next, Jill listed for Dan all the outstanding traits she had taken for granted in him. And she apologized again for her failure to express to him how much those qualities meant to her. Jill's agenda led her to the best part of her ceremony. Not only did she ask Dan to forgive her, but she sought *his* help in making *her* changes. What a reversal of roles! And it was long overdue. Jill explained her well-ordered plan for change, but she knew her habits were deeply ingrained. She would need Dan to remind her when she slipped back into her old habits. And when he at times forgot his responsibilities, she would need him to tell her when he would do them so she could avoid the screaming.

Dan was quietly overjoyed. He assured his mom that he would work on his end of things and he'd be glad to remind her when she slipped. They both held to their agreement. Of course they both fell into old habits at times, but their ceremonious commitment to change and their deep love for each other held them steady. They made it! And so can you.

The whole purpose of gaining control over your children is to teach them eventual self-control. You would have had a much easier time as a mother who rarely screamed if you had mastered self-control years ago. What a wonderful opportunity you now have to break the habits of generations! You *can* acquire self-control. By your example as well as your careful teaching, you can help your children master this task and instill a priceless quality into their lives.

■ ■ ■

CHAPTER 8

THE KEY TO HEALING

From our research and experience, one truth predominates: The art of forgiveness is the secret of a contented life. Tragically, there are many mothers who have never considered the need to forgive either themselves, their children, or others for real or imagined offenses. Here's what one mother said:

> I hate to admit this, but most of motherhood has been disappointing for me. Instead of being fun and rewarding, I have more days when I feel trapped by the financial and time restraints my three children cause. I sometimes feel cheated that I am giving the best years of my life to three children who don't want to listen to me most of the time and are eager to disobey. Then I feel like an utter failure and wonder what I've done so wrong that I can even think such terrible thoughts!

No mother wants to feel trapped, caged, imprisoned. Yet harboring unforgiveness will gradually turn a life into a strong fortress of pain built with the iron bars of hurt, anger, and resentment, and fortified with crossbars of guilt and bitterness.

Dr. Foster Cline, a psychiatrist who has studied troubled people extensively, said, "Good mental health depends on living in a constant state of forgiveness!" We would add, "and so does a good mother-child relationship."

There is freedom in forgiveness. Freedom, stability, and self-control in life always accompany forgiveness. A mother must take two steps before she can experience the healing and freedom of forgiveness. What are they?

FORGIVE YOURSELF

A mother's fantasy is to smile at her children as she speaks kind words softly and tenderly, breaking frequently into bubbly laughter. Too often, threats and screams become a mother's reality instead. Julia, whose youngest is now in college, admitted:

> My screaming caused me to feel so guilty. I remember thinking many times during those early years of motherhood, *What am I doing to these children?* I would go to bed with guilt weighing heavily on me, and I can recall crying out to God, *Why did you give me these children? I am just not a good mother!*

Oversensitive mothers quickly become disappointed because they have not measured up to their own expectations. Guilt grinds away in their emotions and thought processes, and they are left with a battered remnant of self-worth. Kari shared how she felt:

> I have a problem. I berate myself and tell myself after each screaming fit that my children will stop loving me if I ever do it again. That causes me to live in a continual state of anxiety and agitation. Of course, I scream again, berate myself, and so it goes.

It is so important to understand the difference between real and false guilt. You *are* guilty if you have done wrong or have broken the laws of society or the rules of living lovingly. If you have hurt your child physically or emotionally, you *are* guilty. You certainly did not intend to, and so you feel awful about it. That terrible feeling can motivate you to begin to change. A major factor in that change is learning to forgive yourself and really begin to love yourself.

False guilt, by contrast, is a feeling based on misinformation—not facts. Because of habits that are rooted in childhood experiences and family practices and beliefs, you may feel that you have done wrong even when you haven't. Were you to see anyone else doing a similar act, you would not feel they were at fault. If you were to name a law or principle that you had broken, you would have difficulty defining it.

For example, a teenager once told Grace that she felt extremely guilty because at the tender age of three she had been unable to stop her stepfather from beating her mother. She even tried repeatedly to harm herself in an attempt to punish herself for being bad. That was false guilt. Her stepfather was guilty; she was not.

Many people cannot seem to find forgiveness because they are, in fact, not guilty. It is correct information that removes false guilt. So, in reading further, be careful to define which type of guilt you feel. Do not rationalize and make genuine guilt seem faultless, and do not berate yourself for imagined wrongdoing. If you aren't certain, ask a friend, clergy member, or counselor because honesty is essential in this process of forgiving.

Some mothers have specific reasons for their feelings of guilt:

Yes, I feel guilty about my children, because I am guilty. I had already nearly raised three children when I divorced, remarried, and—to my horror—two more children arrived on the scene. About this time my second husband took off, and I was left with two young children to support by myself at this stage of my life. Yes, I am angry—angry that I married another bum, that I was foolish enough to have the children, that I have no money, and that I have to work full-time again to eke out a living for the three of us.

I guess I retaliate by working the graveyard shift, although I don't have to. In that way I see my children as little as possible, since they're usually in day care or with assorted baby-sitters. When I am with them, I often need to sleep. If they don't let me sleep, I really scream at them, reminding them that if I don't get my sleep, I'll lose my job, and then where will we all be? My children, now ages six and nine, are having terrible problems at school. Both are failing academically and socially. The older one acts out his anger, and the younger one withdraws into his own fantasy world. My life is a mess!

This mother's confession screams of her own inner anguish—her helplessness, loneliness, remorse, and daily lashing out at the children, who symbolize her own life pattern of disillusionment. She feels guilty, and she *is* guilty. The good news for her (and others like her) is that she can change. By forgiving herself, she can regain her self-respect. By forgiving her ex-husband, "the bum," she will no longer resent his traits in the children. Through these steps of forgiveness, she will be able to love herself and her children with new depth.

Forgiving ourselves is the first step. Once we accomplish this, we are able to take the second step.

FORGIVE OTHERS

Some of the mothers in our interviews have reasons not to forgive—legitimate reasons. They have been abandoned, rejected, abused, and wronged in a variety of ways. They have lived with enormous hurt and pain, some for many years. Perhaps you, too, have good reasons, understandable reasons, for not forgiving your children, spouse, parent, or significant others in your life. Staying angry seems to offer protection against further hurts.

However, you must forgive if you want harmony in your home. The price tag for unforgiveness is too high. Festering hurt leads to anger, resentment, bitterness, and depression. If any of these are not admitted and dealt with, they will begin to affect your relationships with those around you, including your children, causing physical as well as emotional problems.

Many mothers erroneously think that if they bury the hurts and the pain, those hurts will mysteriously disappear in time. Nothing could be further from the truth. Time does *not* heal all wounds. In fact, if the wounds of life are repressed in the hope of getting rid of them, the opposite will happen. These wounds will grow until at last they emerge with far greater intensity and potential for destruction than they initially had. Hannah More, an English author of the 1700s, understood this. She wrote, "A person will find it cheaper to pardon than to resent. Forgiveness saves the expense of anger, the cost of hatred, the waste of spirits."

It is also vital to understand that the act of forgiving another, whoever it might be, is really more for the benefit of the one doing the forgiving than for the one who needs to be forgiven. Forgiveness enables us to be whole and in control of life and our reactions to circumstances. When unpleasant situations come up that cause hurt and anger, we can immediately choose to forgive. By that supremely powerful act of the will—making the choice to forgive—we come to be in charge of our lives. It is through exercising self-control that we learn to forgive.

To experience healing through forgiving others, a mother needs to take action. Here are a few steps you can take:

Release the Other Person by an Act of the Will

Pat knows all too well what it is like to endure stabs of humiliation and receive the mortal wound of rejection. Over a period of time, her pain from various experiences gradually turned into anger, which she denied even to herself. She can recall mornings waking up angry, with rage fomenting inside, not really aware of where it had come from or why.

As she went through each day, something or somebody would often remind her of a particular hurt. She would mentally take the incident out of her memory bank, go over every single detail, remember each word and action, and relive her feelings of pain and helplessness. All this was done with a maximum amount of self-pity!

Although she was consumed with her problems, endlessly going over what she wished she had said or done at different times, she longed to run away from her angry and destructive thoughts. But where could she go?

At this precise time, when she felt there was no hope and no way of escape, God showed her that the answer to her restless anxiety, grieving pain, and unrelenting anger was forgiveness. She began her arduous journey into forgiveness by first realizing that it didn't matter if she was right and the other person (or people) wrong. She had to forgive by an act of her will and make a conscious choice to forgive. Pat continues,

> I began to repeat, "By an act of my will, I choose to forgive
> _____." Each time a hurting episode flashed
> through my mind during the day and night, I would think, *By
> an act of my will, I choose to forgive* _____ *for doing (or
> not doing), saying (or not saying) that to me.* Complete forgive-
> ness did not come quickly for me. Over and over again, I had
> to choose to forgive the person (people) for specific acts.
>
> Slowly, the process of continually choosing to forgive began
> to work changes in my heart and life. I became calmer on the
> inside. A change of attitude followed, and I became more posi-
> tive. I also began to feel much better about myself—stronger,
> more in control, with a greater sense of worth and joy. All this
> was a surprise! I had no idea the act of forgiving was so powerful.
> Now I can tell you that, at least for me, there is no adequate way
> to overestimate the strength, healing, and freedom of forgiveness.

Release Others from the Responsibility of Meeting Your Needs

Diane shared this story with us:

> I've learned a little about forgiveness. I grew up expecting to
> marry a man who would take care of me in the style I grew up
> with and make me happy for the rest of my life. I married when

I was young. Because of my father's position, we had been afflu-ent. My husband had no money, and I encouraged him to go to work for my father. My father died several years later, and the business went steadily downhill. *How could my husband do that to me, to the children?* I wondered constantly. *How dare he lose the position, prestige, and money that my father had and that I had enjoyed and expected?*

I became depressed and blamed my husband for everything that had happened to us. I also let him know that he was respon-sible for my happiness, or lack of it, as well as everything else.

Years later I came to grips with the fact that I should never have pressured him to go to work for my father. He was ill suited for the business from the start. Slowly, I forgave myself for that initial blunder and forgave him for not being like my father. I also recently have begun to realize that my husband is not responsible for my happiness; no one is. That comes from within me. It's a whole new approach for me to accept responsibility for my happiness, rather than blaming my husband. But I'm learning.

This story reinforces the fact that it is only as we learn to accept ourselves that we can honestly accept others. When we learn to take responsibility not only for our actions but also for our feelings, we will be able to practice acceptance of others.

View Others As Tools of Growth in Life

This story tells how three bites of Jell-O spelled disaster for a family but eventually resulted in forgiveness, healing, and growth:

It was the evening of my husband's birthday. We had been mar-ried for a year and were having a family dinner with my hus-band's children. We have a rule at our home. I serve small por-tions of everything, and if a child wants seconds, that's fine, but the child must finish what is on the plate. It was a rule we made as a family, and the children know it well.

My eleven-year-old stepdaughter asked for seconds on Jell-O, but in a few moments decided she didn't want to finish. Her father told her she must finish it because she had asked for it. She vehemently said, "No!" Again her father explained the rule, and she still refused. He tried to reason with her, stressing the importance of following through. Still she refused. At that point, because of her poor attitude, he told her she would stay at the table until she finished. There were three small bites of Jell-O left on her plate.

Forty minutes later, she was still sitting at the table all alone. I had cleaned up, sat down, and told her how much easier it would be just to finish the three bites. She looked at me and said in a venomous voice, "I am not finishing the Jell-O!"

At that point, I told her to go to her room. She said, "I am not going to do that." I pulled her chair out, took her by the arm, and maneuvered her through the kitchen. She began to resist strenuously and screamed at me, "Don't do that! You're not my mother!"

I had given so much and felt I had a good relationship. That remark took the stuffing out of me—all the zest and good feeling left. I called my husband and told him what had transpired. He told his daughter to go to her room immediately and never speak that way to me again.

She started screaming and crying that she hated all of us, stomped up to her bedroom, and slammed the door. I also went to my room to get away from everybody. I could hear her screaming at her father, saying things like, "I hate you because you never take my side. You're all unfair to me."

That did it. I went to her room and said, "Young lady, you are 100 percent wrong. I never have and I never will ask anything that isn't fair. You children helped us make the rule about seconds, and you broke that rule tonight. Instead of screaming at everybody and thinking how persecuted you are, take time to think that you did the wrong thing. That's all I have to say." I went to my room.

She did not speak to me the next day. Unknown to me, my husband had told her, "When you come home from school, do your homework, think about all that took place, and discuss your thoughts with me."

The next morning she came up to the sink and said to me, "You probably won't forgive me, but I want to apologize for my behavior. I was wrong. I know we make the rules and need to abide by them. I'm sorry, and I hope that you will accept my apology." All this was said with increasing tears.

I looked at her for a few minutes before speaking and then said, "If your apology is sincere, I will forgive you." Through her tears she nodded yes and put her arms around me. I responded with a hug.

Although it was settled for the moment, I felt a serious breech had taken place. At a later time, I talked with her and told her, "It must never happen again. We are a family that discusses things. If we make a rule, we abide by that rule. If we think the rule is not fair, we must discuss it together." I had forgiven her, but it took me several months to feel as though I wanted to trust her again.

Two years have passed since then. We have never had another problem like that, and my relationship with my step-daughter has grown deeper and stronger.

As is true in so many situations, the real issue was not the obvious one—the eating of three bites of Jell-O. It was a power struggle to see whether the child could effectively manipulate the new environment, which included her father, her stepmother, and a rule established by all of them.

Making an issue out of eating three bites of Jell-O seems ridiculous on the surface. However, an important child-rearing principle is at stake: Say what you mean, and mean what you say (refer to chapter 7 for details). The daughter was testing both the father and the stepmother to see what would happen. This father and stepmother stood united, and the child learned that the parents were a team. They meant what they said when they said it, regardless of her reactions. No wonder this problem never occurred again.

The daughter needed to apologize to the stricken stepmother, and with heroic effort she did. The stepmother likewise had some apologizing to do, and she needed to forgive the daughter for the piercing verbal blow she had received. Left unforgiven, the barbs and ugliness between the stepmother and stepdaughter might have continued and resulted in a permanent breech that would have left all the family members resentful, bitter victims.

Forgiveness is a difficult and lengthy process. However, do not be discouraged. Forgiveness is so essential to living together in harmony that it is worth every bit of time and effort!

Seek Reconciliation with Those Estranged

Grace writes that the screaming that so estranged her mother and herself was a tragic collection of childhood memories. It took years to overcome the broken self-esteem and to build respect and warmth. She recalls wanting desperately to be able to hug her mother, and she couldn't. She wanted her mother's approval but felt she merited neither that nor her love. What a predicament! Grace continues,

> During the pregnancy of my second child, Mother suffered a severe stroke and died at the age of only sixty-three. My son never knew her. Mournfully, I followed my mother's coffin

down the long aisle of the church after the funeral. Each member of my family was thinking his or her own silent thoughts, but I experienced a strangely comforting idea. *The next time I see her, we will at last understand each other!* But that healing did not need to wait until I joined my mother in heaven. I am delighted to share with you how beautifully it did come about.

During a period of training in my psychiatric education, students were learning to use a variety of techniques. One of these was called "The Empty Chair." In this concept, the therapist asks the patient, who has an unresolved problem with another person, to draw on his or her imagination. By pretending that person is sitting in the empty chair, he or she says to that person whatever needs to be said or asked. Then the person moves to the empty chair, imagines he or she is the other person, and makes the appropriate reply.

It was in learning this concept of counseling that I chose to work on my still-unresolved problem with Mother. Quietly and tearfully, I poured out all the childish pain, yearning, and confusion that had been locked away for so many years. When I moved to Mother's chair and began to consider how she would have responded, I was amazed at the emotions and ideas that flooded my consciousness. Suddenly I understood that she had loved me very much and that the screaming was her way of trying to make me into the person she felt I should be.

Mother's methods were wrong, but her motives were right. When I understood those facts, I was finally able to release the pain and forgive her. Now when I think of her, it is with fondness. The old sadness and regrets are gone.

Whether your pain comes from your mother, your children, yourself, or someone else, you too can be healed. Through information, a willing heart, an open mind, and a clear decision to let go of the past, you can experience forgiveness.

There is a simple progression from hurt to forgiveness.

- The first stage is *pain.* Whenever your child rebels or simply disobeys, you are likely to feel the pain of worry or fear. If your child or someone you love lashes out at you, that pain is likely to sharpen to pointed anger or even rage.

- Next, you must set your mind and *will to forgive.* You must be willing to give up the deceptive power and protection of your anger. That will temporarily increase your pain, but don't worry. You will overcome it.

- The third step is to gain and examine all the *information.* If you are to do a complete job of forgiving, you need to know three things: 1) what you may have done to cause hurt, perhaps without even knowing it; 2) what prompted someone to hurt you—maybe he or she reacted out of his or her own pain; and 3) a clear perspective on the whole picture.

- After information comes *understanding.* When you have all the important information, put it together. Once you understand the hows and whys of the problem situation, it is much easier to take the next step.

- And that next step is to *release it.* In a class Grace took, the members discussed just how one could let go of a painful experience, whether it was recent or remote. The leader chose a member who was struggling with the basic issue of forgiveness. Looking directly at him, he demanded, "Bob, take out your handkerchief." Obediently Bob reached for a large, white handkerchief and held it out. "Now," said the leader, "just drop it!" As the large white cloth fluttered to the floor, the silence became deafening. All clearly knew that the very bottom line was a simple act of the will: "I choose to drop this!"

When you have dropped your fear, anxiety, anger, and stubbornness, you will know the release from pain. You, too, can forgive—yourself and others. The healing will set you free to love and to be loved as never before!

And isn't love what life is all about—love and relationships? We hope this book has given you firm ground to stand on and some new handholds for when you feel frustrated. Now it's time for you to take some steps to change your life for the better. We know you can do it. We believe in you!

And the rewards? They will be tremendous—in all areas of your life. Just wait and see.

PART 2

ANSWERS TO THE
QUESTIONS
PARENTS ASK MOST

The shrill ringing of the telephone grated on my spirit as I, Grace, began to relax at 10:00 P.M. My day had begun with a 7:30 A.M. appointment, and I had missed lunch in order to see a grandmother who was concerned about her rebellious adolescent grandchild. Frankly, I was tempted to ignore the raucous sound, but because of the lateness of the hour, I was afraid it might be prompted by an emergency.

This call was not a true crisis, but to the anxious mother who was calling, the problem was distressing. Her preteen daughter had been increasingly moody and anxious. On this evening she had refused to go to the dark basement on an errand and now was refusing to turn out the light in her bedroom.

Only a few days before, the mother of a two-year-old had called me to ask if I knew of any classes she could attend to help her in parenting her difficult child. Most of the time she felt quite confident in her role as mother, but there were days, she confided, when she was so angry with her son's rebelliousness and his testing the limits that she was fearful of abusing him.

I receive countless telephone calls about family matters, and for years I also received many letters asking my advice in response to my former radio program, *You and Your Child.* These have made me aware of the many concerns parents share. While the issues are similar, each is uniquely painful to those who struggle to survive, to cope, and to resolve the problems.

The purpose of this part of the book, then, is to capture in print the practical, to-the-point answers that seem to have helped many people. Since I am both a pediatrician and a psychiatrist, I have focused on the questions where I can offer my unique perspective, since most of you reading this book will never consult a psychiatrist about your child. I've also focused on the questions that are unusual or often overlooked in other books and magazine articles. Perhaps you, too, may find here the one burning concern that confronts you. I hope it will help you and your child.*

---

* Note on gender pronouns: If the question did not specify that a child was a girl or a boy, the authors have alternated the use of male and female pronouns.

■ ■ ■

CHAPTER 9

BABIES, TODDLERS, AND PRESCHOOLERS

WAKING UP BABY

Sometimes when I come home late after a long day at work, I'm disappointed to discover that my three-month-old son is sleeping. I'm often tempted to wake him just to play and be friendly, and I admit sometimes I've done just that. Is it harmful to interrupt his sleep like this? If I don't, I could go days without seeing him when he's awake.

By all means, awaken the baby and enjoy him to your heart's content. He needs the bonding with both his parents, whether they work or not. Dads, for instance, may have a different approach with children, and they can help to balance out what mothers provide. Enjoy your little boy. I recommend that you change his diaper and clean him up. Feed him and play with him, and then put him back to bed.

If one of you works and the other stays home, you may find that the homebound parent is exhausted at the end of the day. Thus, if the working parent awakens the baby, that parent should also take care of the baby's needs (such as feeding or changing the diaper) and get him back to sleep. Realize that the parent at home faces as long and demanding a day as does the working parent.

As soon as a baby comes, spouses should work out a schedule for sharing household tasks. The parent at home should not be stuck with all the childcare and all the domestic duties. If both parents work, then sharing all the chores is absolutely *essential.*

I also recommend that you both be aware of *each other's* need to be enjoyed too. Be friendly and playful together with the child, and then when the child has settled down, make time to keep the romance healthy between the two of you. The best gift you can give your child is a mother and father who truly love one another. But you will have to work hard to keep that love alive. As children grow, it becomes harder and harder for Mom and Dad to find time together. Make such time a regular part of your routine by having a baby-sitter scheduled at least once a week so you can get away together.

BABY TEMPERAMENTS

My second child seemed immediately different from my first the day he was born. Is that normal?

It certainly is normal. In fact, research has even been done on infant temperaments. Doctors Stella Chess and Alexander Thomas studied many newborns, following their lives for years. They discovered that babies are born with nine personality traits, the degrees of which varied from slight to intense. These traits are

- activity level
- intensity level
- distractibility
- predictability
- persistence
- sensitivity level (touch, smell, taste, hearing, speech)
- approach/withdrawal
- adaptability
- mood

Some children at birth are on the low end of certain of these qualities, while others are on the high end, and most are in between. Keeping these traits in mind will help you understand and respond well to your child.

Depending on your own levels of intensity in each of these categories, your child may bring you more or less frustration. If you are basically a low-activity-level person, and your child is highly active, you may find yourself worn out by the end of the day. What's important is that you accept your child as he or she is, adapt the best you can, and teach your child to modify behaviors as much as possible. Meanwhile, keep loving that baby unconditionally.

THE FUSSY, NAPLESS BABY

My five-month-old baby has never taken a decent nap. She'll sleep for half an hour or forty-five minutes at the longest, and after this she is awake for three hours before she'll take another half-hour nap. In between naps she's usually fussy and seems tired. This goes on every day. It's very wearing on me because it doesn't give me a good break to get anything done. How can I get her into a better nap schedule?

This parent has a problem, and it has become a vicious cycle. The more babies fuss and cry and the more tired mothers become, the more tense the mother feels; the baby then feels Mother's tension and cries all the more. You can easily see how this happens, so please do not blame yourself or feel guilty because you have a tense, rather sleepless child.

Sleeplessness in infants can be due to discomfort or what we have commonly called *colic*. Or it can be due to habits or to tension. These children sometimes become a bit hyperactive as they grow older.

First, make sure that there are no physical causes for the baby's sleeplessness. If you suspect that your baby may have a digestive problem, I recommend that you ask your pediatrician to help you. Giving a different formula or adjusting the feeding schedule or giving some medicated drops for gastrointestinal spasms (which may be at least a part of colic) can each be a miracle cure for some of these "difficult" babies.

Second, try to keep yourself calm, relaxed, and as happy as you possibly can, even with this irritable little one. Make the environment of the baby's nursery as calm as possible.

Then, I would suggest this: Do not feel that you have to comfort, hold, or cuddle a crying baby all the time! If you can comfort the baby for five, ten, or even fifteen minutes, that's fine, but then put her back down and get on with other activities for a while. If she is still fussing, check on her and try to comfort her again. If you hold the baby for an hour, and she is still fussing, you will become more and more tense yourself. Let her cry for a time in her bed while you take a break. Then when the baby sleeps, get some rest yourself.

Be comforted, because after a while the baby will quit the crying, and you will be able to enjoy each other, I assure you!

TOILET TRAINING

Would you please review for me your suggestions for toilet training?

Whether you have one child or a dozen, it seems as though every time you face toilet training, it's a new challenge. It is one of the most common problems that I receive letters about, and I'm glad to repeat my advice for this mother.

I urge parents not to feel rushed or anxious. Only children with serious neurological damage fail to master this physical skill, and I find that most problems in toilet training come from overanxious parents. So relax. Watch your child for readiness to begin. Don't go by someone else's arbitrary recommendation that because he is two years old, he should begin toilet training. It simply doesn't work that way.

Certain signs will help you know that your child is ready for toilet training. These are as follows:

- The child has *dry periods of over an hour.* When he awakens dry after a nap or in the morning, the child may be aware that he is ready to begin using the potty.
- The child shows that he is *aware of the process* of urination (e.g., when he looks at his diaper while urinating).

When your child shows these signs, begin educating the child. Set him on the potty. I recommend that you use a small potty chair, not a device that fits onto a toilet. Sitting on the low chair feels safer and more secure for a little child. When the child is sitting on the potty, turn on the water in the bathroom, give the child a drink of water, and even let a little warm water flow over the genital area. Many times that will be just enough to start the flow of urine, and the child will be surprised at his success (and certainly you will be delighted).

Wait a few minutes if this does not work and let him try again. But don't keep the child on the potty so long that he becomes tired or resistant. Let him get up, put him in training pants, or even stay in the bathroom with him while he has no pants on and try again in a little while. If you have the time and want to do it, you may even spend a day in the bathroom, letting the child run about and play rather normally and then catching him when he begins to urinate. With the potty so close, he will quickly get the idea, and many parents have found that this really works quite well with their children. If you don't have a whole day to spend, however, be patient. Keep training pants on the child rather than a diaper. This feels different, and it reminds the child to take care of his wetting in the bathroom rather than letting it happen in the pants.

Above all, avoid scolding and punishment. When the child is

ready, he will use the toilet—unless he is so tense, angry, or frightened that he simply cannot. When he does have success, praise him sincerely. If he has none in a week or ten days, I would recommend that you suspend toilet training until the child is a bit older. With patience and love your child will become toilet trained.

VACATION WITHOUT BABY?

We have a seven-month-old daughter who is our delight. We have planned a one-week trip at the end of this month and have tentative plans to ask one set of grandparents to take care of her for two days, and the other grandparents for six days. She doesn't cry when we leave her at either of our parents, but we are still having second thoughts about leaving her.

I certainly urge young parents to get away now and then. The most precious gift you can give your child is loving one another and keeping your romance alive as husband and wife. I know that time alone is very precious. But at your daughter's age (just seven months), I would advise against a long trip like this. The child may very well enjoy her grandparents for a period of some hours, or even a day or two, but a week is quite a long time for a child of her age. Studies have been done, in fact, that indicate that children under a year of age may become depressed and feel abandoned when their parents are away from them for as long as a week. After about eighteen months, harm is much less likely, as the child seems to understand that people leave and come back. An older child can accept a parent's leaving and can survive comfortably.

Perhaps for this vital first year, you could settle for a long weekend, rather than an entire week or eight days. However, if you do decide to go ahead and try this week away or if you haven't any choice, let me recommend the following. Have the little girl go and spend a night or two with each of the grandparents before you go. Picking her up and bringing her back to her own home will allow her to know that she has not been abandoned and that you will come back for her. As the child then spends longer times with those grandparents, she will be able to tolerate it, I hope, without anxiety.

QUALITY TIME

How much time should a parent spend with her baby and toddler? I'm speaking of quality time during the day. How can parents tell if they're spending too much or too little time with their child?

What is *quality time?* Much has been written about quality time. I think quality time is time that is *focused* on relaxing and enjoying the child. Playing together happily, attending to his needs, teaching and guiding, cuddling and cooing, laughing and talking together—those are things that happy parents and well-adjusted children enjoy. Quality time is time freely given because of proper priorities. Perhaps a neat house will not take a great deal of time, but a deeply cleaned house may, and it can wait. Reasonable meals without compulsion for elaborate or gourmet menus will spare a lot more time for fun with the child. I hope that the quality and the enjoyment of your time with your child will grow as he does.

With more parents in the workforce, quality time has become a way of justifying being away from home for long hours. Working mothers, for example, are told it's the *quality* of the time with the child, not the *quantity* that counts. The best research, however, as cited in Burton White's *The First Three Years of Life,* indicates that babies do best in every way when they are cared for by a parent most of the time up to at least the age of three.

When your child is able to entertain himself for a few minutes, allow him to do so. Place him near you as you work, talk to him, smile at him, and touch him now and then. Such actions will encourage a healthy amount of self-entertainment to balance your focused attention to him.

Remember, if you must work away from home, keep your household tasks to a minimum and spend as much of your time as possible with your children. Find mutually enjoyable activities, play and laugh together, teach and train them well! All too soon they will be independent. *Then* you can clean house, put your career on the fast track, or whatever you like.

If a child becomes clingy and acts frightened, or perhaps withdrawn and emotionally cold, then perhaps the parents are spending too little time with him. In an older child, regression to bed wetting, thumb sucking, or other childish habits may be an indication that the parents' time or the quality of that time is lacking.

However, it is possible to spend too much time with a child. If a child becomes overly dependent and whiny, or acts spoiled, then the parents may be giving in too much to him and building their world entirely around him. Likewise, if a parent and baby come to be at odds with one another and are miserable or tense, they will be better off if the parent gets away and finds a little freedom and relaxation on a regular basis. Then that parent can come back and truly enjoy the child.

EARLY DISCIPLINE

I would appreciate any help you can offer concerning the discipline of a child between one and two years of age.

The key to good discipline of a child of any age is a clear understanding of the behavior of which that boy or girl is capable. And it's especially important to keep that in mind when you are dealing with a very young child.

There is a term that refers to a form of discipline used with toddlers. It is *environmental discipline,* otherwise known as *child-proofing a home.* This means changing the environment so the child cannot get into trouble. It refers to using gates, cabinet locks, outlet covers, high shelves, and other strategies that protect a very young child from his investigative impulses. Environmental discipline helps you avoid constantly saying no to a child. No one wants to hear that all day, so discipline must be creative and preventive. However, sometimes you cannot protect the child and your valuables in this way, and you have to say no.

I have a good friend who is a skilled musician. She had a rack full of very expensive sheet music, and her one-year-old son discovered that music. He loved the bright colors on the covers and would grab then and chew on them. Obviously, that was expensive material for chewing and really not very healthy for the child. My friend could simply have put the rack on a high shelf so that the child could not reach it. But she knew that there would always be music available, so she blocked out an afternoon of time to teach her son to leave the music alone. These are the steps that she took, and I think you will find this will work for you, as well, if you follow up faithfully.

She explained briefly to the child that he could not have the music. She used the word *no* frequently and firmly. When the child began to reach for the music, she moved him away from it and put the music back in the rack. Clearly and firmly she said, "No, you may not have this." She would pull back the child's hand and not allow him to touch it. She repeated this process with firmness and consistency, until finally, after an hour or two, the child understood that he could not have the music. The lesson had to be repeated each day for several days, but the child was well on his way to learning not to touch the music. And he also learned another very important lesson—that when Mother says no, she means it and will follow through.

Parents sometimes ask if it's necessary to swat or spank a little child. I think that's not necessary, though some argue that a firm swat may be less painful than the consequence of a child's touching a hot iron or a stove.

Keep the time you have with your child full of love, laughter, and play, and as you and he strengthen the bonds of love, he will become more compliant to please the parent he loves.

TODDLER SIBLING RIVALRY

My question is about disciplining a two-year-old. How can I guide his behavior to be more kind to his one-year-old sister? If our son thinks we are not watching, he'll kick her, push her, or hit her with a toy.

I have known older children to seriously hurt a younger sibling. And parents' usual temptation is to protect the child that is picked upon. Actually, the more aggressive, older child is the one that may need the attention.

Two-year-olds simply cannot be trusted to play satisfactorily with younger siblings. They usually can't even play successfully with children their own age. They are not really developed enough to do that. They are so busy establishing their own rights and their own identities that they can't cope with the competition of a younger child. This older child desires more time and more attention, especially when he envies the spotlight shining on his younger sister. Don't be afraid to give too much attention to your older child. The parents' attitude in this case needs to become more loving and relaxed, and less worried and critical, and soon the older child will settle down. Parents should, however, provide extra supervision of the toddler until he outgrows his resentment of the baby.

As your son matures, you can try to teach him how to interact with the baby. Help him to hold her for a minute, show him how to stroke her cheeks and help her to grasp his finger. As he discovers the joy of this living "doll," chances are he will stop being rough and learn to be gentle and loving.

DOING IT THEMSELVES

Why is it so important for a child to be moving toward independence?

There are two reasons. One is for the parents' sake and the other, of course, is for the child's. Parents who tend to take the easy route to keeping a child dependent and overprotected can actually stunt the child's development. It may be easier—or they may enjoy doing everything for her—but it is not good for the child. Children are eventually going to become independent. That's what they're born to do, and that is right for them. It is a natural, gradual process, and the earlier in the child's life the parents understand that, and work with it, the better the child's life and the parents' lives will be.

If parents miss the child's instinctive cues that she is ready for the next stage of development, then it becomes much harder to make that happen later on. For example, a child of three or four wants to help Mommy in the garden or help Daddy do the laundry. But believe me, at thirteen and fourteen that child really will not want to do those things. So teach her to help early on and make that experience a happy and pleasurable one. You will establish good habits of cooperation and will create a sense of responsibility in her. Most rebelliousness in the teenage years can be prevented by knowing how to encourage the gradual establishment of independence and responsibility early in a child's life.

Here are some rules by which you might help yourself and your child in that development. First, *watch the child's interests and capabilities as they develop,* and encourage those abilities early. Such a simple thing as the coordination it takes to hold a glass or the child's feeding herself with a spoon encourages her neurological development. It also helps her to feel proud of her independence.

Second, *show pride in the child's accomplishments.* Not only does this teach and motivate your child, creating healthy independence, but it also builds the self-esteem she needs. An example: "Susie, how nicely you dressed yourself. What a help that was to me when I was so busy." Not: "Susie, let me do it. You have that shirt on backwards." As painful as it is, and as much extra time and patience as it takes, let the child do it herself.

Third, *allow your child to suffer the natural consequences of not doing something right.* Experience is the best teacher, and kids can feel pride when they learn by doing, even if they learn by making a mistake and correcting it.

Sharing Among Preschoolers

Is it possible for two- or three-year-old children to play together and share their toys?

Let's break that down into the two-year-old and the three-year-old, because there is a remarkable difference even in that age span. The typical two-year-old is truly incapable of interacting in play with other children. The behavior of two-year-olds really is not very social but quite personal. The two-year-old is testing his own strength and finding out what he can and cannot do. He is competing with everyone, and the motto of every two-year-old is "May the better kid win." He needs to find out who is better and stronger.

There are times when kids need that strength, and times when they need to give in. It is important that we not rush our two-year-olds into social situations that are truly beyond their abilities, and we ought not to demand that they do what they cannot do. Two-year-olds cannot share, because they don't even know what to do with toys themselves. They need the time and the space to learn that. Require the two-year-old to stop hurting other children and do not allow him to grab things away from others. Your gentle but firm intervention when your child is around other youngsters will be helpful for protection and guidance for the future. Gradually teach the child how to share and take turns, so that he can learn to play with others successfully later on.

One of the things that two-year-olds can do very well (and which can help them to learn a great deal about cooperation) is to sit down on the floor and roll a ball back and forth. As you sit down and the child does too, the child will develop a good concept of playing together. That can be an important step in learning cooperation.

Another method for teaching a two-year-old how to play with others is by putting a number of objects together in a container. You as an adult may play with him by putting things in and taking things out of that container. Then invite another child to do the same thing so that he is doing it with someone his own age. These simple mechanisms can help a two-year-old to learn how to play with other little people.

Magically, about the age of three, a child will want to play with other children. By then, children have often learned how to share, how to cooperate in all kinds of activities, and how to play imaginatively and creatively together. You will enjoy your three-year-old's playing with other youngsters.

SHY CHILD

My little girl is three and a half, and I'm sure she is a bright child. She learns things quickly, like a song or a poem, in less than a day. She knows some of her books by heart and can also write part of her name. What worries me is how she responds to other people. If they talk to her, she will hide her face and not answer. Is there anything I should be doing for her?

One of the much-studied, inborn traits of personality is that of the ability to approach or withdraw from new situations or people. Many a child has been labeled shy who is simply inclined to stand back and carefully assess a new situation or person. (Stella Chess, M.D., and Alexander Thomas, M.D., refer to this as the "slow to warm up" child.) Anxious adults tend to push such children socially, thereby creating power struggles which further complicate things.

A shy child needs parents who

- accept her unconditionally and do not try to make her something she is not;
- allow her to choose to approach other persons, rather than pushing her toward them;

- give her less attention for performing and more reinforcement for being a child.

I suggest that when you catch your daughter smiling or responding, quietly and enthusiastically compliment her. Try to find some playmates her age and encourage her just to relax. As you yourself relax, I think you will find that this child will grow to be a loving, warm person.

HAIR PULLING AND NAIL BITING

I want to ask you about my son, age two and a half. He has a bad habit of pulling out his hair, especially around bedtime when he is sleepy. He also bites his fingernails. (I do, too.)

If you run your hand over your hair, you find a soft texture that is rather enjoyable. It is not uncommon for children to like to stroke their own hair, or that of their mother, while they are being rocked to sleep as little babies. Pulling out the hair usually begins in an attempt to keep that hair in his hand without having to raise his arm up while he strokes his hair.

I suggest this for this little boy: Provide him with a soft, silky stuffed toy that he can hold when he is sleepy and while you rock him. At this point in his life he may need a little cuddling and babying. By giving him something that is silky and pleasing to hold while he falls off to sleep, perhaps he won't need to pull out his hair. If he tends to eat his hair after pulling it out, I suggest that you not let him, because it will tend to accumulate in his stomach. Hair is not easily digested, and it can create a problem that could require medical attention or even surgery.

Nail biting is another common problem, and one that is not serious but annoying. On a practical basis, nail biting almost always begins because of rough, uneven fingernails that cause discomfort. As the child bites off those rough edges, he may develop a nervous habit that can become a lifelong habit that is hard to break. The solution for nail biting in little children is to keep the nails smooth with a tiny pair of scissors or clippers or a very fine file. I would rub a bit of cream or lotion around the nail bed and the fingernails to prevent hangnails and rough skin. Clear nail polish keeps the nails smooth. It may break the child's habit by giving a different feel to the nails. Also give plenty of physical cuddling and attention to draw the child's focus outward from himself to his environment. I think you will find that those habits eventually will come to a halt.

Some children are born with greater intensity. If your child pulls his hair or bites his nails when he is upset, you will need to teach him to cope differently. Teach him words to describe what he feels, and help him discover what he needs. If he's tired, he may need to be comforted and rocked. If he's angry, help him to express it verbally or by physical exertion that won't harm anyone or anything. Pounding a peg board, for example, can release pent-up frustration.

Public Tantrums

What can we do when our three-year-old son throws a loud temper tantrum in public? His favorite trick is to throw himself down and scream over some little thing in a store or restaurant. He doesn't seem to respond to threats of what will happen when we get home, but we also have hesitated to spank him in front of people.

That is a difficult situation. Children commonly have temper tantrums. They begin at about eighteen to twenty-four months of age and may extend into the early grade-school years. Most children begin having tantrums out of frustration. They simply reach the end of their resources, and in angry desperation they throw themselves down and cry and kick. That gets their anger out, but it usually arouses the anger of parents. Unfortunately, with those early tantrums children may gain certain benefits, and they learn to have fits in order to get their way. It sounds as if that's what this child is doing. By kicking and screaming, he knows he can embarrass his parents and get whatever he wants.

Knowing that helps you understand how to deal with his tantrums. First of all, make it clear to your child (and at two or three years of age, certainly the child will understand what you say) that he will not have any more temper tantrums in public. Explain this before you go anywhere at all. Tell your child that you will not tolerate his fits and decide carefully what you will do. For example, you could decide that if your child throws a fit, you will leave the store immediately and take him home. That usually is quite a punishment because children like going to stores and enjoy the excitement of being with their parents. You may decide, on the other hand, that a time-out would help. The time-out refers to a short period of time (often one minute for each year of age) spent in a spot designated by the parent. This may mean taking him to the car and giving him a three-minute time-out in his car seat, or just having him sit in a corner of the store for that period of time. Leaving him home with your spouse or a sitter the next time may be another consequence that will help him decide to change. Whatever you decide, be sure to follow through. Children are quick to detect if this is an idle threat or if you really mean business.

Often children simply are not mature enough to handle themselves well in public, and if your child is not ready for such privileges, don't hesitate to get a baby sitter and leave him at home. Above all, do not allow your child's fits to gain him any advantages *ever*. You will be glad that you were firm, and that you went through the inconveniences, when your child finally gives up throwing fits.

WETTING PROBLEM

I'm asking about my son who is four and a half years old. He wets the bed at night if I don't get him up, and then sometimes he still wets. He even wets all through the day unless I constantly remind him to use the bathroom. He will say he doesn't have to go, and then in the next few minutes, he's wet. It doesn't seem to bother him. He

never asks to be changed. I've talked to his doctor, and he thinks my son is just lazy.
I haven't taken him to any specialists.

In this case I would recommend that the mother seek the advice of a specialist, because at four and a half a child who habitually wets may have some special problems (though that is rare). Often wetting is not a physical problem but an emotional one. It may be due to worrisome events in the life of the child. The arrival of a new baby, a move, illness among relatives—all of these events can cause fear, guilt, and anger, a dangerous triad in a child's life. These can cause him to regress and to wet his pants again, even when he has been well trained. Let me say emphatically that this does not mean that it is the parents' fault if the child wets. But parents can help find the solution by understanding the problem and trying these suggestions.

Conflict between the child and his parents is one cause of both bed wetting and daytime wetting. Another cause (and I suspect it is the case of this child) is that a child is so busy and involved in play that he doesn't take the time to go to the bathroom. *He* doesn't mind being wet, so why should his mother care?

There are numerous cures for bed wetting. There is an alarm device that can be ordered from a catalog. This goes off at the first drops of moisture, as the child begins to wet, and by awakening the child can condition him to wake up before wetting the bed; then he can go to the bathroom. However, this is a drastic and rather negative solution, as it is quite disturbing to a child to be suddenly awakened from a sound sleep by this alarm.

Sometimes when children are a bit older and still wetting their pants, the parents may need to put them back in diapers for a while. I recommend that you do this sensitively, without shaming the child, and let him know that when he is ready to use the bathroom, he can stop wearing the diapers. (The type of diapers that can be pulled down to use the toilet are perfect for this problem, as a child can wear them without feeling ashamed.) Be sure that you are not nagging or fussing at the child. Simply explain to your child the reasons for stopping the wetting: It creates an offensive odor, he will be starting school soon, it makes work for others, and so on. Set up a plan with your child, giving him certain privileges that he can earn by staying dry. Set a timer to remind him to go to the bathroom, but do not get into a power struggle if he refuses. Lots of love, encouragement, optimism, and patience will help you and your child through the rigors of toilet training.

LEAVING A CHILD IN THE NURSERY

How do you leave a child in a church nursery? We've tried, and we've already done everything wrong. First, we kept our daughter out of the nursery until she was about a year and a half because she always cried there. Then when we did decide to leave her, we made the mistake of sneaking out. She really threw a fit when she realized we were gone. Now it's really a problem.

That's a common problem, and I spent a number of months working in my own church's nursery, so I understand the other side of that difficulty as well. I have a plan that I have found works a great many times, and I would like to suggest it. You will need to plan to miss the church service for a couple of weeks. You may alternate that between you, as mother and father, but this is what I suggest that you do. (With variations, this works in a nursery or any other childcare facility.)

First, explain to your two-year-old, who will understand a good deal more than you might think, that you are not going to feel sorry for her when she stays in the nursery, that you know it will be good for her to learn to play with other children and to give you the freedom to attend the church. Whatever your explanation, make it very clear— you are *not* giving her a choice but explaining your decision.

On the other hand, let her know that you certainly understand her fear of the strangeness and that she will miss you and want to be with you. Now when you go to church with her the next time (after you have given this ceremonious explanation to your child), take her with you to the sanctuary. Let her see where you will be sitting and then walk with her from the sanctuary to the nursery. Knowing the exact route will give her a little more security.

When you place her in the nursery, do not act ambivalent. If you are unsure about leaving her, she will pick up on that and will be unsure herself. Leave her the first time (after your talk) for as short a time as two minutes. Leave her, telling her that you will be back in a very short time. Then return to her promptly, so that she knows you will follow through and that you will be back. The next time you leave, make it five minutes, and gradually increase the time that you are away. Consistently returning to her will help her to know that she is not abandoned, that you *will* be back, and that you are reliable parents.

You will, of course, need to make the nursery supervisors aware of your plan so they can cooperate with you. I suspect they will be more than glad to have such a plan working, rather than to have a screaming child for an hour every Sunday. The following week, I recommend that again you go through this leaving and returning process. Within three or four Sundays, I can almost guarantee that you will find that your child will be staying in the nursery happily playing away, and you may attend church with absolute peace of mind.

■ ■ ■

CHAPTER 10

SCHOOL-AGE CHILDREN
AND TEENS

AFTER-SCHOOL ACTIVITIES

I suppose that many parents who work away from home would be interested in your opinion about how much supervision a ten-year-old might need during the time between the end of school and when his parents get home from work. Do I need to get a sitter (which my son doesn't want) or can he manage on his own?

Before I answer that specifically, I would like to share a story of an actual case that I worked with. One of the schools in which I used to consult was having a major problem with a fifth-grade child. He was getting into a great deal of trouble at school, and children were coming to school and reporting problems that he created in the neighborhood. When we called his mother to come in and talk with us, she was indignant and assured us that it couldn't possibly be true that her son was behaving badly after school. She told me that she always insisted that her son telephone her as soon as he got home, and in talking with him she was convinced that he was just fine. What she did not realize, of course, was that after the son made his call, he was going out and creating trouble.

A child of ten or eleven cannot be assumed to be able to get along without you. If possible, I recommend that one of the parents be home within a few minutes of the child's arrival. If it is impossible, here are some suggestions that can help you decide what to do in providing the proper supervision and protection for your children.

Evaluate your neighborhood. Know who lives next door to you and even around the block. Is yours a reasonably safe community in which children can play together outside with the supervision of other neighborhood parents? Are there children who could influence your child to get into trouble, or who would be ready partners in mischief your own child created? Are your neighbors friendly? Are they at home much of the time, and would they be available in case there was an emergency or some need?

Evaluate your child. Is your son truly responsible and honest, or is he, as most children are, capable of being deceptive when he thinks you don't know about it? Is he easily tempted to mischief, or is he a responsible child with plenty of things to do after school (such as homework, practicing an instrument, or using a computer)? If he uses a computer, will he avoid the many damaging opportunities on the Internet?

Evaluate your job. Does it allow you and your child to contact each other if needed in case of a problem? Would you be able to leave on the spur of the moment if necessary?

If several of the above conditions are such that you feel concern for his safety, your child will have to bow to your good judgment and accept a sitter. Don't overprotect your child, but do protect him enough to keep him safe. Fortunately, more and more schools are adding before- and after-school care to their programs, and many community agencies also sponsor childcare for older kids with activities that are more geared to their interests.

SUMMER CAMP?

Many of us have wonderful memories of attending summer camp, but watching your child wave good-bye from the window of a moving bus is a terrible experience. Is camp a good experience for children?

I think summer camp is a wonderful experience for children, but it does need some good judgment and planning. Usually camp is something good, but there are children who suffer severe attacks of homesickness and have difficulty adjusting to the large numbers of children, the scheduled activities, and the new adults who supervise them. In order to find out if your child is really ready for summer camp, here are some questions that may help you:

Is your child ready to go? Just because all of the other kids of a similar age are going off with excitement that does not mean your child is ready. Be careful to ask him honestly, without overprotecting and without pushing your child to go. By the age of nine or ten, almost all children can go to camp for a week, and they will really enjoy it. That doesn't mean that *every* child is ready by that age.

Has the child had a previous experience being away overnight? If an overnight visit with a friend has been an unpleasant or frightening experience, the child may still have some fear that could make going away difficult. If a child does not enjoy overnights with friends, he or she is unlikely to enjoy and entire week away from the family.

Is the child afraid that you want to be rid of him? Does he think you will give extra attention to a brother or sister while he is away from you? Find out the camp's policy regarding phone calls home or parental visits if the child becomes very homesick. Some camps are lenient, and others are very strict. If the child can call home, be positive and reassuring when he does, rather than sympathetic and rescuing.

What is the camp program? Does it offer activities that your child really likes and is good at? Or does it emphasize areas of life that your child doesn't particularly care about? If you have a lurking fear that camp this year may not be good for your child, then wait. There's always another year, and perhaps next year will be a far better time.

Finally, whenever you are choosing a camp, be sure to pick one with an excellent reputation. Churches, YMCAs, and Scout troops are good sources of information about camps. Find out how counselors are trained and what sort of screening they go through before they are hired. College-age kids with a background in child development and several years' experience in camping are likely to be better counselors than young high schoolers with little training. Find out about the facilities and be sure that there's plenty to do. Some camps may be less expensive but turn out to lack facilities and can be boring. If money is a problem, request information about scholarships. Scout troops, Ys, and churches often offer scholarships to deserving children.

VIDEO GAMES

Do you think that playing video games is harmful to children?

I do think they can be harmful to some children, as negative effects can result in

- isolation—many video games are not social activities;
- neglecting better activities, such as reading, chores, educational pursuits;
- violence—many of the games are actively violent;
- intensity—children often seem lost to the world while they play.

If you do get video games, select those that develop skill and coordination without violence. Limit the time spent on games, alternating them with more active play. Watch your children for ill effects, and if you see them, don't hesitate to weed out the video games that might be a cause of those problems. Some children become obsessed with video games, using them as an escape from family troubles or difficulties at school. If you have a child who is constantly glued to a video game instead of socializing with family or friends, you need to make an effort to reconnect with that child and find some more meaningful pursuits for him or her.

However, video games can also be positive influences for

- family interaction if parents join in the games;
- developing hand-eye coordination;
- attracting friends—again, with games for more than one.

If your children's friends come to your house to play video games, you can get to know them and how they interact. That's a positive outcome, as it's good to know their friends.

Video arcades are quite a different matter from video games played at home. Such arcades can be undesirable places. A great many drugs are exchanged in public game rooms, alcohol is common, and tobacco smoke is so heavy that one's eyes burn.

I also feel concerned about the money that children spend in such public arcades. There seems to be a compulsive need to play just one more game, with an almost excessive sense of excitement or tension with such activity. Undue competitiveness is a common part of many of these games. Some people argue that this is good, as it allows children to play out their aggression so they do not take it out on their brothers, sisters, or playmates. But such competition may stimulate aggression outside of the arcade.

Violence

Do you know the effects of television or video violence on young children? My husband and I have four children, ranging in age from two to nine. If you could give me some insight into this subject, I would appreciate it very much.

We in the mental-health profession are concerned about the effect of violence on children. For many years studies have indicated that violence does influence young children. One group of school children in California was studied a number of years ago after they watched violent scenes, and then they were observed as they played afterward. The children who had watched the violence had a great deal more intensely violent situations among themselves than children who had not watched such scenes. Recently we have learned that even cartoons can have this sort of effect on children. And in the case of cartoons, kids may get the idea that death and injury are not real because cartoon characters get blown up and are perfectly fine a minute later.

I think parents must closely monitor television programs for children younger than seven or eight. At this early age, children do not have the capacity to determine right from wrong adequately, and they simply do not understand what is good or bad about the cartoons they watch. As you watch television with your child, forbid the violent, destructive programs. Your children will survive without a great deal of television, and there are almost always a few good programs that you can permit. Even with those, I suggest that at times you watch with your children, reinforcing the positive ideals and views portrayed and helping them to understand any questionable views or any ideals that are contrary to your own. Kids need to know the truth.

If you are appalled at the kinds of programs that go on the air, write to your local stations or to the programs' sponsors, expressing your views and clearly defining what you see as harmful in those programs.

PREPARING FOR ADOLESCENCE

How can we avoid problems with our teens during adolescence?

It is in the adolescent years that the cracks in the foundation of a child's personality become clearly visible. It was, however, the family foundation of the early years that contributed to the damage. There are three primary reasons for serious adolescent misbehaviors:

1. *Parents are too rigid or strict.* When parents are dictatorial and maintain too much control over too long a period of time, young people are likely to rebel in order to establish a semblance of independence. Since the job of teenagers is to do that very thing if they are to become healthy adults, parents must not only allow but *encourage* them to grow steadily toward independence, in order to avoid serious rebellion.

2. *Parents are too lenient or inconsistent.* Teenagers need to have their boundaries enlarged, but they still need boundaries. When par-

ents do not establish such limits or enforce them erratically, adolescents will test them regularly. The more inconsistent the parents are, the more strenuously the young people must test their limits. To stop dangerous behaviors, parents must begin to set limits and enforce them with great consistency.

3. *Adolescents carry too much emotional pain.* When teenagers feel very inadequate or carry anxieties and worries that are too heavy, they often act out such painful emotions in wildly erratic behavior. By doing drugs or carrying out antisocial acts, they can temporarily escape their pain. They may even set themselves up to get caught and punished, because punishment temporarily relieves their guilt. Such young people need a chance to explore their needs and to verbalize those painful feelings, so they will not need to act up.

Understanding teenagers is fundamental to staying in love with them, enjoying them, and seeing them through those difficult years.

Music Videos

Our daughter is in her early teens, and she has started watching cable TV stations that air rock videos. Should we be concerned about this?

Yes, indeed! Cable stations that show music videos sometimes air material that is extremely suggestive of violence, explicit sex, and drug abuse. More and more we see physical abuse depicted, accompanied by rap or hard rock music. While these stations also air music videos that are well done and tasteful, a parent cannot know which type a child is watching unless the parent is watching, too.

I suggest that when a child becomes interested in music videos, a parent watch along with her. Discuss what you see. How does she feel about the scenes of violence or sex or drugs that are portrayed? Is she sensitive to words and pictures that demean women, authority figures, ethnic groups, or the government? In this area, a parent must try to stay informed. Once you have pointed out the poor values in the music videos, then you can tell your child that she should not watch them unless you give explicit permission or are watching with her.

ROCK CONCERTS

You have a lot of contact with teenagers in your work. What is your opinion on rock concerts and rock music in general?

Many parents are deeply concerned about rock music. A great deal of rock music has to do with promoting the highs of all sorts of drugs along with violence, illicit sex, and crime. Also, each year new methods of exuberant celebration come around, such as "moshing" and "surfing," which have caused a number of injuries and deaths at concerts, parties, and "raves." Parents must try to be informed about these. Many teens are in a desperate search for intense excitement and a means for expressing profound inner anguish. This and the need for social interaction can drive a teen to seek out these exhilarating experiences.

On the other hand, there is some fine contemporary music that has no bad words or criminal influence. In fact, this may be a bridge for many young people from negative, destructive music into more wholesome music and renewed faith in God.

What kind of music your teenager should listen to and whether or not your child should attend a rock concert are certainly important decisions you as parents must make with your child. Get complete information about the group that your young person wants to hear. Be careful that you have accurate information before you make a decision. Being too rigid can prompt your teen to rebel; being too permissive can invite destructive influences. Find a balance.

Fortunately, there are more and more Christian groups available whose music appeals to teens. Concerts featuring such groups are likely to be better supervised. Yet even then it's best if your younger teens only attend if an adult is going along.

REBELLION OR INDEPENDENCE?

How can parents tell if their teenager is rebelling or just trying out a new idea?

There are some very specific guidelines that can help parents to differentiate between open rebellion and experimentation.

Attitude. A truly rebellious teenager almost constantly has a hostile, sarcastic, or cynical attitude. She is secretive over prolonged periods of time and becomes manipulative and tricky. It's hard for the child or parent to really trust one another if she is a rebellious teenager.

Behavior. Not only is the teenager's attitude important, but so is her behavior. The committed rebel is potentially destructive in the things that she does. If not destructive in the sense of physical damage, the rebellious teenager is destructive of herself as a human being. She does things that disqualify her for trust or respect by other people. Rebelliousness also is generalized, and includes rebelling in school by not getting the schoolwork done. There is also rebelling socially by misbehaving, sometimes in serious ways, rebelling at home by not following the rules, and refusing to attend church. Across the board there is a resistance to the rules or expectations of the family and society in general.

Resentment. That is another one of the characteristics of rebellious teenagers. As parents examine themselves, I find that many of them discover that they have been too rigid and controlling for too long a time. Extreme control and severe punishment both contribute to resentment.

The child who is going through a healthy search for independence will argue over specific ideas or values or rules. She needs to argue in order to stretch her own growing intellect. She needs to be listened to and argued with, in good humor, in order to develop her self-respect and establish her real beliefs and values. But this child will soon return to her basic goodwill and love for her family. Studies show that parents are the most important influence in a teen's life. So keep your influence positive and strong.

Teen Finances

Our high schooler needs to develop financial responsibility. She works part-time, and we're wondering what expenses she should contribute to. Also, how can we get her to keep financial records? Should we expect her to budget?

Once these parents are basically agreed on financial values, then they can arrange a kind of business meeting with their daughter. Discuss the following issues openly and frankly, but kindly:

First, what are the daughter's expenses and the family's? What is the cost of living? What are her future plans? Is she going away to college, or does she plan on some special job training? Does she want to buy a car or get her own apartment? What are the costs of all of these rather major things that children sometimes want a few years down the road? Discuss together how she can best prepare herself for those future plans and what you parents can and cannot do to help.

Next, help her outline a simple budget and then put the information in an accounting book or on a computer program. If she is not going to college or into some other special training, then I think she should begin contributing to the family budget, saving money, and planning for her future.

If she is mature and responsible, you could put her in charge of all her own needs. Supplement her income if you need to, and help her figure out ways to pay for all her clothes, transportation, meals, and so on. Encourage her to set aside savings and a tithe for church or charity before other needs.

Keep this positive and helpful, and avoid disapproval or blame. I think you will find that helping a child manage money will also teach a great many other values for successful living.

TEENAGE DISCIPLINE

How should parents respond when a teenager has done something that's really wrong?

First, the parents need to *verify the facts.* You will lose your child's respect if you jump to conclusions, assuming he is wrong when perhaps he is not. I will never forget the time we had a call from the police station about our adolescent son and his friend. We were told that they had been caught shoplifting from a local store. But when we went to the police station to check out all of the facts, we discovered that it was a case of mistaken identity. It had not been our son at all.

Second, if you do know that a wrong has been done by your child, *cool it.* Simply do nothing until you get control of your emotions and can handle the situation with wisdom and caution.

Third, sit down with your child. You, the child, and any other significant people can *discuss the situation* in private. I recommend that you not question the young person if you are certain that he has done the act. Asking him direct questions will often add to the problem by prompting him to lie about it. Review with the child what was wrong with what was done. Be sure that the child understands what he did, why it was wrong, and how it might hurt a number of people as well as himself.

Fourth, *wait for the child* to recognize the wrongdoing and want to make amends. It is one thing for you as parents to know that it's wrong. But it will not help your child to grow in maturity and understanding unless *he* knows what was wrong about it. A friend of mine endured immense grief over a serious act of vandalism by her teenage son. He refused to admit it, but she learned undeniably that he had done it. After much thought, she took a long book to read and went to his room. "Neither of us will leave this room until you have told the truth," she said matter-of-factly. She then sat and began reading her book. Two hours later, her son finally revealed the facts. Together, they worked out a way for him to remedy his act. He was relieved, and learned a lifetime of lessons in a single day!

Fifth, *set up a consequence* that will be meaningful to your child. It should be one that will help him to see the seriousness of the act and to prevent a recurrence of the problem.

Finally, *look for any underlying reasons* for the misbehavior. Perhaps the child had a valid reason for what he did that you were unaware of. Or perhaps he is seeking attention or acting out some worry or anxiety. If serious wrongdoing is repeated frequently, I urge you to seek counsel that will help diagnose and cure such actions.

BIRTH-CONTROL INFORMATION

Would parents who feel very strongly about sexual morality be encouraging their teenagers toward promiscuity by telling them about contraceptives?

That's a question that a great many parents have asked. By the time their children become teenagers, parents should have taught them a sense of morality. By that I mean what makes a particular act right or wrong. They should have given their children a set of values to live by and have taught them how to understand their sexuality and control their impulses, how to be sensitive toward each other, and how to act responsibly in social and dating situations. If that moral teaching has not occurred prior to adolescence, parents will have some work to do very quickly.

Most parents intuitively know when their children are becoming interested in sexual practices—they have reached puberty and are expressing an interest in the opposite sex. If you have not already done so, this is the time to discuss sexual activity with your child. Your child needs to know how he or she is allowed to relate to the opposite sex (e.g., "friendships and group outings are okay, but no actual dating yet") and why. But don't stop there. Talk to your child specifically about what sexual behaviors you feel should be saved for a later age and what should be saved for marriage. Make it clear, for example by citing research and Scripture, why you feel the way you do about intercourse before marriage. But don't be too negative. Also teach your teens that sexual intimacy is a beautiful, fun, and even sacred experience. That's a big reason why it should be saved for the person one marries for life.

However, you must also be realistic. If you have raised your child to share your moral values and you have not been overly rigid, then you can be assured that your children will, deep down, have a desire to live up to your expectations. But you must take into account the impulsivity of the typical teen, the pressure for early sexual activity in some social groups, the desire for rebellion in some cases, and even the frequency of date rape. You have to communicate to your children why you have serious concerns about sexual activity. Then I recommend that you also talk to them about pregnancy, sexually transmitted diseases (STDs), and contraception. And be sure to talk to both daughters *and sons* about these issues.

Contraception is a very controversial topic, and there are many in Christian circles who feel that any talk about contraception will encourage sexual activity. But I do not agree. If contraceptive information is given by you, in the context of a strong set of moral values, I believe it will give the child the information needed without encouraging sexual activity. You can stress that the only guaranteed protection against STDs and pregnancy is abstinence. There are a number of social groups now that encourage abstinence, such as the True Love Waits movement.

Parents, be careful that you not become so rigid that you push your children in the very direction that you want them to avoid. One of the saddest situations I knew was a young woman from a conservative home who was pregnant out of wedlock. When she explained to me how it was that she had allowed herself to become sexually active, she told me that her mother had been so strict that she simply had to rebel in order to prove to her mother "that she can't boss everything I do."

On the other hand, you should not be so laid back that you fail to make your moral values clear and fail to give your teen the information he or she needs to make informed decisions. Providing no information is as bad as giving a child the wrong information. They both lead to poor decision making.

If you believe your teen is sexually active, I suggest that you thoughtfully and prayerfully sit down with your teenager. If you have a healthy, open, and affirming relationship, you can ask why he or she is becoming sexually involved. Does she know what needs are being fulfilled? Has he been under strong pressure from peers? Is there a fear that she might lose her boyfriend if she does not go along with his sexual advances? Does he feel his girlfriend expects him to make advances? Have there been parties with alcohol or other drugs and a high level of sexual overtones? Try to help your adolescent understand and try to understand what he or she is dealing with. Perhaps you can help your teen get needs met in a more wholesome way. In fact, teach your teens how to plan such fun activities with friends that they won't think about having sex. Also teach them to recognize sexual arousal and to set boundaries to control it.

If, on the other hand, you do not have the kind of open relationship that would allow such a discussion to take place, then you are in a much more difficult position and probably have little influence on your child's behavior. If your teen is sexually active, get him or her as much information as possible about contraception and protection. Be sure to include both subjects, as many forms of contraception do nothing to protect someone from a sexually transmitted disease. Offer to take your rebellious child to the doctor or a clinic, pay for the visit, and foot the bill for contraception and protection. If you can do this calmly, while still making your own moral position clear, it may be the beginning of a return to a more open relationship between you. And, as always, pray for guidance for yourself and a change of heart for your child. (True Love Waits even has a specialized program for those who have been sexually active but want to be abstinent again.)

UNDERSTANDING TEENAGE PREGNANCY

From your experience with pregnant teenagers, what would you say a girl in this situation needs most from her parents?

Interestingly, one of the most important aids that a pregnant girl seems to need is the help and support of her father. She needs her mother, but during this time somehow dads are especially important. In working with a great many teenage pregnancies, I found one of the common denominators of them was an emotional distance from their fathers. In fact, many studies indicate that estrangement from her father is a major factor in becoming intimate with a man. So, Dad, you need to spend time with that daughter, even though it's a sensitive time in her life. This can give her a chance to understand herself and her relationship with her boyfriend, because many times that boyfriend is symbolic of you as the dad. Many children (and so often they are really children at heart) do not know why they become sexually involved or how it was that they allowed themselves to become so irresponsible. Here are some points that you need to understand in this regard.

Many times young people's involvement in sexual activity comes from their need for *someone to love* them—someone to prove to them that they are desirable and someone to belong to. Other young people are trying to *prove their sexuality.* Women may have a need to feel feminine, and their boyfriends to feel masculine. Some young girls even desire to become pregnant. They think that having a child will give them someone to love and *be loved by.* The desire to gain *attention* from their parents and especially from fathers is a major subconscious (and perhaps even a conscious) part of the needs of these young people. Searching for tangible evidence of love is a common denominator in the young people who become sexually active.

From these needs and inner feelings of teenagers, you can see that what daughters need most from you is love, acceptance, forgiveness, the security of your definite commitment to them, and the will to make sense out of a difficult situation while growing in responsibility.

AMBITIOUS TEENAGER

My high schooler loves to be a part of everything (class officer, school play, athletics, and more). He does carry responsibility well, but I'm wondering if I should help him say no. How many extra activities are good for a teenager?

Perhaps I can answer that by saying that only those activities that teach him to be a better person or allow him to serve or help other people are the ones he should pursue—assuming that he also does some things just for fun! I suggest that young people limit their extracurricular activities to two or three besides school and church.

Help him formulate his priorities and his philosophy of life. Most thoughtful parents would like their teen to focus on being well rounded. This might entail being in groups that include the following six types of activities:

- *Character growth.* Activities that encourage this need to be at the top of the list. Reading the Bible, being involved in service groups in church or the community, or joining a charity can be a wonderful means of growing spiritually and developing healthy character.

- *Emotional awareness.* I also think that young people need to be involved in activities that increase their awareness of emotions—their own and others'. Most group activities, in that they require getting along with others and negotiating problems, can help teens understand interpersonal dynamics.

- *Creativity.* Your child needs to develop his sense of imagination and creativity. Any task that can help your child discover unique talents and abilities is important. Many extracurricular activities such as band, orchestra, the arts, yearbook committee, and so on, focus on creative pursuits.

- *Intellectual development.* Though this tends to be focused in school, students also benefit from enrichment at home or else-where. Thus, you might want to encourage a child to be exploring various computer games, searching the Internet for answers to questions (with appropriate adult supervision), or participating in a math or literature quiz group. In addition, many of the things a child does in creative pursuits or service projects require intellectual skills.
- *Social interests.* Your child needs to be in some activities that will help him learn to get along with a variety of people, rather than sticking with one particular crowd. Girl Scouts and Boy Scouts often capitalize on this, trying to form diverse groups of kids and help them get along together.
- *Physical development.* Promoting physical development is the same as promoting good health. If your child has gym daily at school or is generally an active child, you don't need to worry so much about this. But kids who tend toward being "couch potatoes" would benefit from some sort of regular exercise. This can be as unstructured as a family game of badminton or as structured as a community soccer program.

Finally, make sure your child knows that *fun* is a valuable activity that is absolutely essential to life. And having fun means having enough free time to play. Time to play, think, imagine, meditate, and just exist, is what each of us needs and many of us don't get. Help your teen to think through his priorities and choose activities of the right sort and number to promote personal growth.

PARENT-TEEN COMMUNICATION

My fifteen-year-old son is going through what I call the "grunt" stage. It just seems so hard to get him to talk about school or girls or anything. He'll have episodes when he's very open, but in between, silence. When I ask too many questions, he thinks I'm prying.

That letter reminds me so much of my own daughter. When she was fourteen years of age, she and I were really at odds with one another. I changed my working schedule so that I could be at home when she got home from school. I had the juice and the chips (or whatever I thought might appeal to her) handy, and the stage was set for us to have a wonderful time of communicating. Unfortunately, that just did not happen. I would ask her how lunch was that day, and I would get, like this mother, a grunt. I would ask how a test was, and I got another monosyllabic answer, one that I couldn't really interpret one way or the other. Before long, she was off to her room and all chance for communication was lost. I was hurt beyond measure, because I loved her very much, and I felt her slipping away from me.

Fortunately, I asked God's guidance and that of a great many friends and came to an understanding of what was going wrong. As a matter of fact, my daughter herself told me. She said one day, "Mother, you are absolutely yucky! You ought to know that I am not four years old, and you can't talk to me like you did when I was four. I'm fourteen." And to her, fourteen was pretty old. Even though she sounded a bit rude, I understood what she was saying, and I quit trying to talk to her as if she were a child. I looked through my days desperately for any event or subject that I thought would be of interest to her.

The next day after school, over a soft drink, I said, "Kathy, let me tell you what happened to me today." And I told her a story that was somewhat funny. It was a miracle, because I hadn't yet finished the story when she said, "Oh, Mom, did that really happen to you? Let me tell you what happened to me." And we were off to a major change in our relationship.

Judaism has a marvelous ritual. It is called the *bar mitzvah* or *bat mitzvah*. At this time young people celebrate the transition from childhood into the adult world with a religious ceremony. The children know rather clearly when the child stops being a child and becomes a young adult. In non-Jewish families, we can develop this transition, much as I tried to do with my daughter. It is largely a state of mind, although some people choose to develop a ritual or celebration around it. My invitation of my daughter into adult life was sharing with her the events of my days and treating her like an adult.

Share feelings, events, and thoughts with your child. I think you will find that he in turn will share with you. Express interest without prying. Understanding your adolescent is so important if you are to grow to become adult friends in the years to follow.

SHOPLIFTING

How serious or common is the problem of teenage shoplifting?

The problem is very common, and unfortunately it is not limited to teenagers. There has been a great rise in shoplifting even among the elderly in our society. Many stores now have store detectives to pick up those shoplifters. If I were a parent who had a shoplifting teenager, I would be grateful if he got caught the very first time around, because getting caught can create a healthy fear and honest respect for the law.

Perhaps more important than what a parent is to do is understanding why kids shoplift. One of the reasons is that they are craving excitement, and somehow it becomes a bit of a cat-and-mouse game. "Can I get this bit of makeup?" or "Can I take the flashlight without anyone realizing that I have it?"

Testing the limits of authority is another reason for young peoples' stealing. Pitting their cleverness against the mentality of the large stores or shop owners is a challenge. Very rarely do these kids need the items that they are stealing.

The most common shoplifters are those from affluent families. They seem to need attention, to be noticed, and that prompts many misbehaviors, including shoplifting. Almost always, in my experience, the habitual shoplifter feels unloved, unimportant, unattended to by parents or other significant adults. This does not mean the parents actually do *not* love them; the kids just do not *feel* that they are loved.

Some thieves are unsuccessful people who somehow feel that they can achieve a sense of importance through shoplifting. A great many young people also steal to support drug habits, and that's a very strong motivator.

If your child has been caught shoplifting, require that child to return the item at once. If she has used the item or damaged it, so it cannot be returned, require her to earn the money to pay for it. Evaluate your family, including yourselves; see if your teen is getting enough attention and positive affirmation. If not, take steps to begin to correct this. Also check out her friends. See if any might be a bad influence on her. And remember, mistakes are forgivable—by you and by God. Make sure that your child knows that.

DANGER SIGNS

What are some of the signs that would tell parents that their son or daughter had a very serious emotional problem or was becoming suicidal?

Each year there are a number of young people who will commit suicide or attempt to do so. In many cases, they could have been stopped if their parents had known these signs and responded appropriately:

- *Physical signs.* These are the first and easiest to define. These signs include a major departure from the child's usual physical patterns, such as a change in eating habits. This may mean the child who has normally eaten fairly regular meals begins eating excessively or nothing at all. It can be either extreme, and that is important to observe. The same is true of sleeping. A child may sleep excessively or a decreased amount. *Any major change* is worthy of your notice.

- *Social signs.* The teen may withdraw into his own room and his own little world. He may escape into excessive activities in order to avoid emotional pain. He may become rude and irritable or extremely polite. Again, it is the variation from that child's own unique norm that is worthy of consideration.
- *Emotional indicators.* Any marked change from the child's normal status should be noted: a child who becomes irritable when usually he has been fairly mild mannered; depressed when he has usually been happy; excited when he has usually been quiet; unusually worried, anxious, or moody. All of these are signs to be noted.
- *Personal habits.* These also need looking at. Giving away special treasures, leaving a will or notes that seem to be accidentally left around, or deterioration of work at school—these are all signs that can help parents to know a child is sad, angry, or in danger.

I hope that you will be aware of your child's behaviors in all of these areas of his life. Do not hesitate *if there is any concern* to seek the advice of a competent family counselor. Get the help that you and your child may need—before it is too late! Your troubled child may clam up and act like he doesn't want to be bothered. Do not be deceived by this! Without lecturing or nagging, be persistent. Say, "I can read the worry and sadness in your face. Please tell me about your concerns. There's no problem our love and God's wisdom can't solve." Give him a bit of time and space, but stick with him (or her) until the problem is solved!

■ ■ ■

CHAPTER 11

FAMILY RELATIONSHIPS

HOME ENVIRONMENT

If you were to describe the perfect home environment for children to grow and develop, what factors would be most important?

What a wonderful question! Here's what I would advise:

1. Work on the marriage. Having two parents who respect and love each other is a major positive factor in children's lives. Parents, be sure that you communicate respect for one another in front of your children. Love is wonderful, but it is not very helpful unless it is communicated clearly, consistently, and honestly.

2. Give unconditional, loving acceptance. Accepting each child for exactly who he or she is constitutes another essential factor in a secure family life. Approval and disapproval must be communicated in a positive fashion, so that support, encouragement, and cooperation are common.

3. Offer appropriate correction and discipline. These are essential for children to grow in their self-awareness, in interacting successfully with other people, and in learning a sense of compassion for others.

4. Provide a congenial atmosphere. Make wholesome laughter common in your household. Be careful, however, that your laughter is never ridicule of someone else.

5. Involve extended family. One of the most secure things in my childhood was my extended family. My grandmother lived with us until I was a senior in high school, when she quietly passed away. Her presence was an influential factor in my life. The uncles, aunts, and cousins that surrounded us also were comforting in times of illness or distress. Helping your child to know your extended family can require special planning in today's mobile society. But telephone calls, letters, and visits can give your children that sense of being a part of generations. The extended family will help them to feel the security of belonging to something larger than themselves.

Not all extended families are positive influences, however. Some family members are negative, overly critical, judgmental, or even abusive or alcoholic. If this is the case, then the children will not benefit from frequent exposure to these family members. Instead, help your children to love these family members, to enjoy the good in them, and to recognize their failures in order to avoid repeating them.

6. Show hospitality. Make your home a welcoming place for your children's friends. This will be a springboard for their becoming healthy adults and a place for returning when they need a shelter as they grow older.

Pressured Dad

My wife and I want to do the best job possible of raising our daughters, and we try to spend a lot of time together as a family. But one thing that really bothers us is that while people expect my wife to make changes in her life for the girls, a man isn't supposed to. My friends at work don't seem to understand why I don't hang around the office any longer than necessary. A couple of guys even have said that I am hurting my future. But I feel as if I'm doing a good job and not cutting corners on my work. Do you have any suggestions?

Studies in recent years show that fathers are key figures in the lives of both girls and boys. So this father is right to fight for time for his family.

My first suggestion is that you try to get a sense from your supervisor or boss about whether taking on extra projects is expected for promotion or for maintaining your current job. Without talking specifically about family concerns, try to come to a clear understanding with your boss so your mind can be at rest. Most bosses will respect a desire to identify job expectations but many will not be able to accept a father's saying that his family concerns have the potential of affecting his work.

Be quite certain in your own mind of your priorities. Then you can take the jibes of your friends without letting them bother you. I have talked to many men and women who have turned down major advancements in jobs in the interests of their children, and I respect that immensely. Such determination and courage portray to me real strength of character, wisdom, and great love. It is not as necessary to advance in your job when your children are small as it is to advance the interests of your children themselves. I cannot emphasize enough what a major influence fathers are in the lives of their children.

EFFECT OF DIVORCE

My youngest son, age twelve, was only eight when his dad and I divorced. Sometimes I wonder what the long-term effect will be. Do you have any suggestions?

Either directly or indirectly, divorce affects a majority of American homes. There are many feelings involved in every divorce—grief over the loss, anger over the rejection, all kinds of very intense, negative, and destructive emotions.

Children are especially vulnerable to those feelings. They rarely get those feelings worked out, because they don't know how to talk about them. They don't have the vocabulary to express them, and their parents are so involved in their own distress that they are often not aware how urgently the children need to deal with those problems.

Fortunately, there are now programs run by schools, churches, and community groups that seek to aid children of divorce. Rainbows is one such program. It aims to help children talk about the divorce, recognize that their family is not alone, and build new hopes for the future of their two families. These groups can be especially important for children during the early months of the divorce or separation when emotions in the family are running high and the parents may have difficulty talking calmly about the events in the family.

Recent studies emphasize the importance of fathers as well as mothers. Long-term studies of divorce indicate that the outcome for the children depends largely on how well the custodial parent (if parenting is not shared) handles the divorce and whether the noncustodial parent remains connected and in tune with the child. If your child's father is not involved with your son, then a substitute "dad" or "big brother" would be a good influence. Look among your male relatives, neighbors, and church members to see if you can find someone trustworthy and emotionally healthy who might act as a good buddy for your son. The Big Brother program in many communities links willing adults with boys from single-parent homes.

Once some of the divorce turmoil settles, parents can discuss the topic of divorce with less emotion. Help your child to talk about things that upset him about the divorce. Are there living or visitation arrangements that cause the child grief? Are there questions about the past, about the circumstances of the divorce? He might not remember much about that time in his life. You might be surprised how little he remembers. Encourage him to talk about his feelings and concerns. He is old enough now to be able to begin to put his feelings into words.

Here are a few more important ideas for helping any child of divorce:
1. Make sure he understands enough about the divorce so that he does not blame himself. (But give no sordid details, please!)

2. Give him permission to love the other parent. Don't try to make him an ally in your divorce battles.

3. Teach him to forgive others when wrongs are done (and work on forgiving your ex-spouse yourself).

4. Be sure not to allow him to manipulate you by using the other parent.

5. Help him to identify the good in both parents and avoid seeing only the bad.

MAKING A WILL

We're in the process of drawing up a will, and we want to include a statement about who should take care of our minor children if something happens to us. We're wondering if it should be someone in the family or friends who share our interests and have similar lifestyles. Also, would it be better to choose people who already have children?

This is a wise couple. Though making a will is a painful process because no one would like to anticipate his own death, it is a necessity. There are several goals that parents need to consider in developing such a plan for their children.

1. You want your children to have the security and familiarity of their own environment. Unless the children are very young, they should not have to face losing their familiar surroundings as well as their parents. Ideally one would select guardians for them who are close enough that they could continue attending their familiar schools and church. For some families that plan would necessitate the selection of relatives. For others, the neighborhood, the school, the church, and so on could best be maintained by selecting friends who live nearby. For very young children, the consistency of caretaking is much more important than maintaining the same environment. But if you name a guardian three states away when your first child is

born, you should be prepared to change your will as your children grow and enter school.

2. A second consideration is the values that you deem most important for your children. Whom do you know that will teach these same values to your children? Again, for some of you this may be relatives. For others who do not share the same values as your relatives, you may find friends could best maintain that goal for your children.

3. Further, you should consider the ability of the couple to manage children. Though Grandma and Grandpa may have been excellent parents for you, will they still have the youth and energy required to raise another set of children if you name them as guardians? Or should you select someone younger but childless? I believe that couples who have their own children can usually understand and adapt to other children more easily than people who have had no children at all. So, this is something to consider.

Whomever you choose, I would recommend that you do this by formulating a plan. Cultivate those people as friends. Spend time together so that they and your children will get to know, love, understand, and trust each other. If there are major differences or a lack of respect, it may help you decide to choose a different family. Offer a simple explanation of your plan to your children, so they understand who this special family may be in their lives, but avoid worrying your children or making them fearful of losing you.

PREPARING A CHILD FOR A NEW PARENT

What guidelines do you recommend for getting a stepparent-stepchild relationship off to a good start? My three-year-old daughter will soon have a stepmom in the house.

Many parents and children are facing new relationships due to divorce or bereavement. The issues that are at stake are these:

- Her father's time and energy will now be focused on the new spouse.
- The child may feel a sense of displacement or rejection.
- The new spouse may feel rejected if the child does not take naturally to her.
- The child may feel disloyal to her biological mother. (How can she love a new mommy when she still loves her old mommy?)
- The new mother will bring changes in lifestyle and family routines.

Handling these issues is not simple. Try keeping these principles in mind as you attempt to build a positive relationship between stepchild and stepparent.

Give information. Explain and explain and explain again! Do not take for granted that the child will understand the new living arrangement and the advent of a new mommy. Help her to know that she doesn't have to choose between her "old" mother and the new one. She can love both of them and treat them each in her own way. Sometimes this process is helped along by choosing a name for the new mother that does not compete with the "old" mother. If a child can distinguish the two by name, then she will feel less disloyal to her biological parent.

Keep an open mind. The stepparent should not expect any specific behavior but should explore who this child is and what the relationship can be. She should think about what she has to offer this child and what the child has to give to her.

Identify the good points. What are the good points about that child's biological parent? It's very easy for a stepparent to subtly compete with a child's absent mother or father and to find out bad things about him or her in order to appear better. Avoid that at all costs.

Understand that child's losses. The child is probably feeling grief, confusion, and anger over the loss of a parent in death or divorce. The child will often tend to cover sad, tender feelings with aggression and acting out in a rude and unkind way. By understanding the child's tender feelings, anxieties, and concerns, the stepparent will not feel personally affronted or hurt by the child's misbehaviors or her reluctance to accept a new parent. Instead, help her through those difficult feelings by labeling them and interpreting them.

Focus on unconditional acceptance. Concentrate on kind, honest, and complete acceptance of the child. That doesn't mean the stepmom must put up with rude or disrespectful behavior but that she understand the child's honesty with her and accept that. Encourage the child to talk out the feelings that she has for the stepparent, as well as for her natural parent. Treat the child as you would a dear, young friend.

Earn respect. Do not expect an immediate parent-child relationship; work toward earning that while developing a friendship. The stepmom should allow the child to approach her and should be available, but she should not demand a sudden intimacy or response because that simply cannot happen. Move slowly into parenting. Any changes in rules should be explained in detail to the child by the biological parent.

Expect divided loyalty. Manipulation can occur when the child tries to play her parent against the new person in the house. If you expect this, you will be ready to handle it by refusing to compete with the other parent, by not tolerating the child's manipulations, by staying together as adults, and by working together for the child's sake. Tough as it is to create a new family together, both you and your child can do it.

PRIVACY

What guidelines would you offer parents on the subject of children's privacy?

There are three major factors that I think can help parents understand the need for privacy and how it changes with age. One is the *age of the child*. The second is the *child's personality,* and the third is the *mood or the circumstance of the moment.*

Age. Prior to the age of six or seven, children rarely need privacy.

Up to three or four years of age, a child needs to always be within sight or hearing of an adult. But after age six or seven, a child begins to need some time alone in order to become an independent individual. By the age of ten or eleven, a child's needs for privacy increase greatly and they continue increasing through the teenage years.

Personality. Some children are extroverts and need and want very little privacy. On the other hand, the introverted child enjoys and needs much more time alone.

Mood or circumstances. Privacy needs also relate directly to the current circumstances and mood of the child. Some children, when hurt or angry, want attention, hugs, and comfort from their parents. But others need their "space." They need time to cool down and figure out their emotions a little bit. Such children demand parental ingenuity and sensitivity. Recognizing and respecting the child's need for time to think through anger or hurt is very important. Later on, you can go to the child's room and knock on the door and see if your child is ready for a hug or a talk. If not, keep returning at intervals until she or he is ready.

CHILDHOOD GRIEF

My husband and I have two sons, three and a half years and eighteen months old. We recently had a baby who was stillborn. Our oldest son was truly excited about the new baby. The loss of the baby had many effects on him. He has begun wetting his pants, sleeping and eating poorly, and behaving unpredictably and rebelliously.

This certainly is a family crisis. Death is the ultimate loss with all of the helplessness and sadness it causes in the survivors. It's very difficult for adults to deal with death and can be more difficult for children. The stages of grief, as formulated by Elisabeth Kubler-Ross and others, are important to review briefly: First, there is denial that it has actually happened, then a sense of loss, anger over that loss, and finally, preoccupation with sadness, pain, fear, and guilt, that go along with all grief. Eventually, however, healing does come!

A child facing a family member's death will probably experience fear as well—fear of the adults' grief and his own pain; fear that possibly this death is a punishment for some of his naughtiness; fear that he might die if another child could die. A child certainly is going to feel angry, and this anger covers up his pain and fear. His rebellious behavior is simply acting out the anger he feels. The following steps are recommended to help a child deal with grief:

First, *explain as much as you can.* Help the child understand that it is not his fault. You don't have to defend God and try to make the death look okay, either, because at this time the child is not going to believe that or feel it.

Second, *be honest.* Admit that you do not have all the answers to the child's feelings or even your own at this time.

Third, *be reassuring.* Make sure your child knows you love and accept him, even in the midst of his regressive and unpleasant behaviors. Baby him a great deal and give him the comfort of your physical presence frequently.

Fourth, *encourage emotional expression in appropriate forms.* Help him to put his fear and anger and guilt into words, if possible, or to express them on a pounding board or in tears. Cry with him, if you feel like it, and comfort him.

And yes, *allow your child to participate in the visitation and/or the funeral.* I recommend that children attend the funeral home and view the casket and the body, if possible. The ceremony of a funeral is one way of expressing grief. Being there to see the person who has died and knowing where the body is helps us all to complete that grief process in a concrete way. Also, more and more funeral homes are putting together special programs for children who are grieving. Check with your local homes.

Grief and loss are facts of life. You and your child can and must learn to cope with and transcend it together.

PARENT-CHILD DIFFERENCES

What kinds of family problems grow out of personality differences between a parent and child?

A great many problems can develop. A pediatrician in New York City a number of decades ago began studying parents and children from birth. She followed as many as possible for a number of years, and her discoveries are worth thinking about. She found, for example, that when a mother who was placid and loved peace and quiet had a child who was energetic and into everything, she developed a problem with that child almost from birth. Resentments began to grow between them that became lifelong and serious in their impact. On the contrary, she found that a mother who was energetic and active might have a child who was very peaceful, quiet, and introverted. She could become impatient and troubled about such a child, and set the stage for discrepancies and resentments that create disharmony in the family.

I find many times that parents love to cuddle babies, and yet some babies don't like to be cuddled. They squirm or stiffen and simply will not relax and settle into the mother's arms. That can cause resentment. A mother may fear that somehow there is something wrong with her as the mother or that the baby doesn't love her. Unconsciously, animosity and power struggles may grow that will set up the parent and child for serious problems later on. One mother spent her years of motherhood feeling cheated because she did not have a child with the temperament of her dreams!

Here are some simple rules for living in harmony as a family: *Define your unpleasant feelings toward your child.* Whom does she look like, or what is it that she does that creates problems for you? Make peace with the person she reminds you of (or work on your anger and grief if the child reminds you of your former spouse), and reconcile yourself to those traits as a gift of God to your child.

Then, *learn to accept and love her as she is.* Unconditionally, give that child the attention and the love that she needs in the way that she can best accept. As you affirm your child, you will build up some hope for her worth and success. You will see that child bloom, and you and your child will grow together.

Baby-Sitters

When Mom and Dad can't be home, do you see any problem with hiring the high-school girl next door to take over?

There is nothing wrong with leaving the children with a sitter *if* you have carefully checked into that sitter's abilities and maturity. There are instances of sitters who have abused or failed to protect children in their care, and you don't want that to happen.

Be sure to screen baby-sitters carefully before hiring one. Here are some criteria by which you might judge a good, reliable sitter. The sitter should have:

- A high level of maturity
- Good judgment in times of crisis
- Enough self-control to never slap or yell at a child
- The ability to control and discipline a child
- Willingness to avoid socializing with peers while sitting
- References that can attest to all of the above

You must give your baby-sitter clear guidelines about the kinds of discipline that you use and that you would want her to use in case it is needed. The baby-sitter needs to have judgment enough to know when to call you and what she can handle in case she cannot reach you. The basic love of children and the ability to be kind and firm and protective are qualities that I would look for in a baby-sitter. I'd like to have a baby-sitter who is energetic and willing not only to provide basic care, but to play with my child so that the time they spend together is enjoyed by all.

How can you know what a baby-sitter is like? I recommend that you request references and call those references to talk with them personally. I suggest you have a sitter spend some time with your child while you are there, and observe carefully what goes on between them. When your child is old enough, ask him or her how the evening went after the sitter is gone. Observe carefully the condition of the house, the sitter, and the child when you return. If you have concerns, come back unexpectedly and pop in on the sitter during the course of an evening out. It may be an inconvenience, but it may serve a good purpose in helping you to know whether you can entrust your child to this person. Trust your instincts! If you have a sense that something is wrong, don't leave your children with that sitter again until you have investigated.

Another suggestion that I have is that you might trade baby-sitting now and then, so the cost doesn't become prohibitive. Several couples who are trustworthy friends can relieve one another and thus provide some special time out. And, of course, there are grandparents. The good ones are worth their weight in gold. I know that I love to keep my grandchildren when my daughter goes out!

HOLIDAY PREPARATION

How can we make family holidays really special?

The following elements are important for holiday experiences, and unfortunately it's very easy to unknowingly miss them all.

Mood. I like to try to set a mood of general congeniality. The goodwill that is so essential to holidays is vital in the family as well. Smiles, laughter, and jokes are important all through the year, but holiday time is a natural time for such goodwill and happiness, as well as tempting secrets and surprises. The inclusion of children in the decorating, baking, and other preparations is sometimes a bit of a trial to a busy mother, but it is also a part of the happiness in building family traditions.

Rest. Holidays should also be a time of quiet and peacefulness. Take time out personally and as a family to be quiet and to look at the decorations and enjoy the anticipation of gifts.

Meaning. Meditate on the real meaning of the holiday, such as God's gift of his Son to our world. And thank God for the other gifts he gives us, such as good food, warm houses, and families. The ultimate expression of holiday sharing is in the free gifts of God. (If you're worried about how the secular holidays may affect religious meanings, try to be clear with your children. I know of one family, for example, that celebrates "Bunny Day" on Saturday before Easter. That leaves Easter free to celebrate the resurrection of Christ.)

Tradition. Building traditions is so essential! Every Thanksgiving we have a similar menu for dinner and breakfast. At Christmas, we had familiar tree ornaments, which we have saved from time immemorial, and each year the children and I enjoyed unpacking those ornaments and using them on our traditional tree. Reviving old customs and recipes, which perhaps your grandparents enjoyed, might be helpful to your children in valuing their backgrounds and learning from whence they came.

■ ■ ■

Chapter 12

Discipline and Spirituality

Inconsistency

How can my husband and I avoid being inconsistent in disciplining our children when we don't always agree on what our family rules should be? How will inconsistency affect our children?

Predictability is one of the basic emotional needs that all children have. But you cannot be consistent as parents until you are reasonably united. *That's* where you need to start. Talk and negotiate until you do come to an agreement. If that demands the outside help of a counselor, don't be afraid to seek that help. At least in your basic policies you must be in agreement. The best results in child rearing involve clear, reasonable, and meaningful guidelines enforced consistently, day after day.

When the disagreement involves minor matters, it's quite all right to let your discussions teach your child how to be honest and to disagree lovingly and discuss constructively in order to reach a successful compromise. In major matters, however, such disagreements create a climate for manipulation. I know one family in which the daughter has learned repeatedly to go to her father for things that she wants, because he is a softer touch than her mother. That has created resentment, guilt, and fear among the members of that family.

Here are some simple guidelines that will help spouses in establishing consistency with your family. First, *identify goals* that you want to reach for and with your children. How do you want her to behave? What do you want her to achieve in life? When you think about those goals, it will draw you together, because there is no question that both moms and dads want the very best for each of their children.

Once you have set those goals, *plan the methods for reaching them.* That demands that you establish some basic policies and rules for your family. It also implies that there must be teaching and modeling of the qualities and values that you are talking about. Decide which parent can best enforce each rule. In some cases, the mother may be far more effective, and in others the father may be. Each one must take the lead in their best areas, *but back one another up in a consistent, united fashion.* Working for consistency is not an easy task. It will be well worth the struggle.

SPANKING

Many child specialists recommend that parents not spank children. But others say this is permissive and that children should be spanked. What do you think?

Many years ago I began to realize that even the most loving parents, under enough stress, can cross the line from punishment to abuse. This has prompted me to rethink my attitudes toward spanking.

Advocates of spanking quote the old proverb (Proverbs 13:24; 22:15 and others) about sparing the rod and spoiling the child. I always believe the wisdom of God's Word. And God's Word talks about the rod and staff of a shepherd. Let's look at what that means.

As a girl, I often tended my father's sheep. If they strayed into the wrong pastures, they could die. My job was to stay constantly alert. If one sheep headed for the wrong pasture, I would gently prod him with a stick. It took relatively little poking to get him back where he belonged. A beating not only failed to work, but it often created anger and could draw an attack.

In my five decades of work with children, I have rarely, if ever, seen this philosophy fail: Parents must stay watchful at all times and firmly and lovingly guide their kids into safe pastures. If you are considering spanking a child, ask yourself these questions:

- What do I want my child to learn about life and avoiding errors? (In other words, what is the point I'm trying to make? Will it be made by a spanking?)
- What is the *least* painful consequence that will teach these lessons? (Strict parents often err on the side of overpunishing a child. In general, a little punishment goes a long way.)
- How can I follow through with consistent guidance?

I think that you will find that gentle, firm restraint, timeouts, and the loss of cherished privileges, along with your appropriate disapproval and boundary tending, will eliminate the need for spankings.

How to Avoid Spanking

Our son is almost four years old, and we're trying to use spanking less often as a form of punishment because we were spanking him almost every day. But we're having a hard time getting away from it, because that seems to be all he'll respond to.

Spanking does, of course, allow for the alleviation of guilt through suffering pain over one's misdeed. Often, however, spankings do not stop or change the pattern of a child's misbehavior. They simply allow the child to feel free to misbehave again!

My parents were very strict people. My father was the authority in our family, and obedience was demanded. However, I can recall only two spankings in my entire life. When I hear of a child who is getting spanked every day, I feel sad, because I know there is a great deal of tension and ill will in that family.

In good discipline the parent must be creative. One time my father got me up late at night to go outside in the cold and darkness to do a chore I should have done when it was lighter and warmer.

That taught me a very important lesson. He did not lay a hand on me, but I got the point, and the irresponsibility changed. That's a nice example of how to discipline creatively. Giving a child extra work, making him clean up a mess or fix what was broken (or at least *try* to) can help that child to learn a more important lesson than he would learn from a spanking.

It doesn't matter if the child seems to enjoy a consequence that you give him for misbehavior. Even if he hates sitting in a chair for a time-out, he is going to pretend it's a game in order to convince you that it doesn't work. Then you will resort to the punishment he's looking for—a spanking! If you put a child in his room and he does not stay there, simply continue taking him back to his room each time he comes out, saying, "The timeout will begin as soon as you stay in your room." Eventually, after many repetitions, he will learn that you mean business, and he will stay in his room.

The general guideline for timeouts is one minute for every year of the child's age. But I have some guidelines that I like better because they require the child to take responsibility for what he did. I suggest saying, "You will stay in timeout until you can tell me what you did that was wrong, what you should have done instead, and how you will handle it the next time."

But this is not the only form of discipline available. Grounding a child, limiting television, making him go to bed a little early, giving him extra chores, are all ways to teach a child that certain behaviors simply will not be tolerated.

Don't worry about the consequences not being serious enough. If a child breaks something and has to clean it up, you might not feel it is punishment enough, especially if the object was expensive or full of memories. But you have allowed your child to amend for his error by cleaning up after himself. And when you do this consistently, he will begin to be more careful. Then the cycle of carelessness and spanking will stop.

CONSEQUENCES

What discipline and consequences would you suggest for lying and bad language?

This is a common problem even for God-honoring parents who don't do these things. First, discover why your child is lying or swearing. The most common reasons are to gain attention from peers, get out of certain duties, or make themselves feel important.

The child who lies or swears is nearly always insecure and lacks a healthy self-confidence. As you step back and evaluate your parenting, you may discover that you have been too harsh, perhaps a bit inconsistent (letting lies work now and then), and that you have not balanced your punishments with enough love and congeniality.

Start the discipline, then, by changing your patterns according to the need. Be firm and consistent, but keep a caring and kindly attitude. Your child will learn even more effectively from kindness if you follow through.

Do make it clear that lying will not be tolerated and that there will be consequences. For example, if your child tells you she has cleaned her room when she really hasn't, go with her to clean it at once and allow her to miss playtime or delay her dinner until it is done.

For swearing, I suggest a child pay a fine for each unacceptable word. This fine may be taken out of his allowance, or he may be assigned a job to earn the money owed.

Be sure to explain clearly why these habits are harmful and that it is out of love that you are punishing him. If you really mean that, your child will recognize your concern and, sooner or later, he will comply.

FORGETFULNESS

Other than constant nagging, what can parents do to help children remember things?

In order to avoid nagging, simply rely on natural consequences. That is, if the child is late to meals, the family goes right ahead and eats, and whatever part of the meal that child misses, he misses, until the next meal comes along. You do not rewarm the food, you do not extend the mealtime, you do not rescue the child. Likewise, if the child forgets to take his lunch to school, he goes hungry or begs or borrows money in order to get lunch. That's one lunchtime that he will remember—perhaps the next day when he is starting out the door again without a lunch.

Be sure you praise your child's good qualities and reflect on those so that he does not feel like a failure. If your child is forgetting because he is thinking about something worrisome, try to find out what it is and deal with it.

Finally, some kids just have more trouble than others remembering details. Often these children have ADD or another learning disability and cannot help themselves. They need understanding and strategies for success. Here are a few ideas:

- Write a list—on a piece of paper, on a calendar, on a dry-erase board on the bedroom door or on the refrigerator.
- Use a watch with an alarm to remind the child of appointments.
- Write up checklists to enumerate all the steps in a process (e.g., a checklist of things one must do and items one must pack before leaving for school).
- Avoid nagging so your child will not learn to get by on your sense of responsibility. Let natural consequences teach him.

Every child will benefit from strategies that help him or her to be more organized and responsible.

CHEATING

It was very upsetting and embarrassing when my child's teacher called and said he had been caught cheating. Why is it that some children just give in to the urge to cheat, even though their parents have stressed honesty and playing by the rules?

Frankly, the motivation for most cheating is understandable and positive. Children cheat because they want to do well, and every parent and teacher wants the children to do well, too. The problem is that they have somehow learned how to do well without putting in the honest effort that it takes to learn the material. Interestingly, most cheating begins quite by accident. One child sees another do it and get away with it. The opportunity then presents itself to him, and in a moment of weakness, he gives in and finds that he has done quite well because he cheated.

The payoff has seemed to teach the child that cheating is worth it. Grades get better. *I can get by (the child reasons) without putting in so much work, and so why not do it?* Our society, in fact, teaches us to look for easy ways. There is a bit of natural laziness in all of us that really prefers to take the easy way toward success.

The important thing, once parents understand something of why the child cheats, is understanding what to do about it. Having worked in schools for some twenty years, I am appalled at the number of parents who take exception to the reports of misbehavior. Often I find parents taking the child's side, even when the child is clearly doing something wrong. Your first step needs to be to team up with the school or the person who has become aware of the cheating.

Watch your own child carefully. See if he wins by cheating when he plays games with brothers and sisters. See if there are other little evidences of dishonesty that begin to grow. When you see these, do not ask the child if he is doing them or why he is doing them, because he will promptly deny them. But do reveal to your child what you have seen. Explain to him that these things are dishonest, they will not be tolerated, and then set about changing his behavior according to these steps:

First, *check your own lives.* Your children will be quick to pick up your example, so if you have not been completely honest, work hard to shape up your own lives. Second, explain to your child directly that you will not tolerate cheating and dishonesty. *Set up a consequence* for any time the child breaks a rule, whether at home or at school, and follow through with those consequences. (Work with the teacher for consequences at school.) Finally, *praise* your child for changing that habit. *Correct* him when he does not, and you will win this very important issue.

EMOTIONAL BLACKMAIL

How should parents answer when their children try emotional blackmail?

In my experience, a child blackmailing a parent is symptomatic of the child's having accumulated too much power in that family. It is the *parents* who should have the power. I think many families today have reversed the old parental role in which my father, for example, would say, "If you don't do this, Grace, then this will happen," and I knew it would. Today I'm hearing children say to their parents, "Mom, if you don't let me do this, then I will run away," or whatever. That's a very frightening situation for the child as well as the parents.

Let me give you examples of *what not to do:*

- Do not act worried or upset, because that may imply that you believe the child has the power to do what he is threatening.
- Do not counteract that child's threats with pleading. Be strong; act as an adult and do not try to get the child's love or happiness back too quickly. Dealing with the situation is far more important than keeping your child happy all the time.

When you face an emotional blackmail: First, *clarify what the issue is.* Why is the child threatening and upset? What is the problem? When you find this out, talk about it. For a younger child, you may need to put into words the child's feelings, because often a child does not have the vocabulary to express that. "I know you are angry or scared [or whatever], and here's what I think you need…" As a parent, when you verbalize what the child is going through, you will help him to calm down and thus alleviate the stress that's making him attempt this blackmail job.

Second, decide what you can do together about the problem. Help the child feel powerful by solving his problem rather than by dictating to his parents.

TEACHING AN INFANT ABOUT GOD

What can a mother do in the first years of life to teach a child about God? Is prayer all we do at this age?

Prayer is an essential element in our child's upbringing. But it is not all we can do to introduce that child to God. The most vital part of a baby's life is the development of trust. That sense of trust in Mother and Father is the quality that is later transferred to trusting the heavenly Father. As the new parents comfort their little baby, provide for her safety, cuddle her with strength and warmth, provide joy and stimulation, and feed the baby, they are teaching that child the basic sense of trust that is so important to developing faith. God designed parents to teach a little child what God is like.

As the child grows, you can sing to her about Jesus' love, read stories about God's care and forgiveness, model God's care and forgiveness for her, and then give him books to read about God.

EXPLAINING GOD TO SMALL CHILDREN

What words would you use to explain God to a small child?

That's a difficult question, because a great many adults do not have a good concept of God. When I give psychiatric evaluations to people, one of the questions I routinely ask them is what they think about God and what God looks like. I receive a variety of answers. To many adults he is a harsh, punishing parent. To some he is a wise, loving, impersonal power. How God enters into your lives as parents determines how you will communicate him to your child.

One of my best learning experiences in understanding God was the time that my father had me watch a baby chick pecking its way out of its shell. He taught me that God is a wise Creator who had a wonderful plan for how things should happen in nature. My brother explained to me how lightning releases nitrates into the soil, and yet lightning and thunder had been very frightening to me. Understanding that they had a purpose made God's power magnificent to me. The cycle of water from the lake to vapor in the air to rain that waters the soil was another example, as I studied science, of God's marvelous handiwork. Walking through fields of wheat or a garden made me aware of the teamwork that humans and God have together.

When you speak to a child about God, try to include these concepts:

- God is loving and warm. When I taught my children this and read them stories from the Bible, I would hold them on my lap and demonstrate to them, physically, the love and warmth of human parenting. I taught them to compare that with God's heavenly parenting.
- God is wise. He knows all things, past, present, and future.
- God is powerful. He can defeat any enemy.
- God is creative. He called all the worlds into being.
- God forgives. There is nothing we can do that can separate us from the love of God. You can help your children to understand this by forgiving them when they have done something wrong.

All these essential characteristics make up a healthy view of God. Children learn these through learning from parents, reading their Bibles (there are many beautiful, simple new versions), and worshiping with other children who believe.

CULTS

Is there a certain type of person who is more vulnerable to the lure of cult groups?

Yes, there is such a person, but perhaps it would be helpful to start with a description of the characteristics of a cult. There are so many new groups springing up around our country today that it is sometimes hard for parents and young people to know whether a group really is basically Christian or a cult. Several of the cultic characteristics that are easily detected are these:

1. *Rigid structure* and unbending rules, usually with one *very strong authority figure.* There is always a charismatic leader, someone who is easy to follow and who is very dynamic. Almost always in today's current cults, this is a man.

2. *Indoctrination or brainwashing* that includes sleep deprivation, lack of privacy, intensive structuring of the entire day, restricted contact with family and former friends, and other mind-control techniques.

3. *Severing of family ties.* Cults (and gangs also) aim to keep followers both physically and emotionally distant from families. The cult group wants to replace the role previously played by family and friends.

There are several types of people who are susceptible to the cults. First are those who are adventurous, exploring types—young people who have their minds open to anything and everything. They may have little discernment or experience and little training in how to make value judgments. These young people, however, while susceptible to cults, oftentimes are also wise enough and strong-willed enough to get out of them.

The second group of people worry me more. This is the type of young person who is lonely and who lacks a close relationship with a parent (often the father). Through the cult such people may seek friends, a sense of belonging, and a father figure. The cult offers such people the family togetherness that they crave.

Another group of young people who are susceptible to cults are those who have low self-esteem, high dependency needs, and a willingness to submit to authority, even if it is bad. People who are compliant and easy to get along with adapt well to cults.

Every parent and young person needs to be able to recognize the characteristics and structure of exploitative cults today so they are prepared to avoid them.

SUNDAY-SCHOOL DROPOUT

What can you do if your child doesn't want to go to Sunday school? My eleven-year-old son says that it's boring. His class seems to be fine and the teacher is good, so I'm baffled about my son's resistance. Will I be helping him any if I insist on his attending?

The reasons children should attend Sunday school are fairly obvious. We want them to learn about God, his Word, and his world. We want them to see the importance of the church and its function in their lives and the world in general. And we want our children to make friends with those who share our spiritual values.

There are also several reasons why children resist going to Sunday school. Some, unfortunately, resist going because they want to reject their parents' values or win a power struggle. Also, children are often influenced by their peers to think that Sunday school is kid stuff for "wimps." And Sunday school is, sometimes, juvenile or irrelevant if it is not geared to the specific age or needs of children. Sometimes children have stayed up too late the night before and are too tired to get up for Sunday school.

Today's children are spoiled by having so much entertainment available to them. They come to believe that everything should be entertaining and exciting, and Sunday school just can't always be that.

Whatever the reason, parents should be clear about the value of Sunday school and explain those reasons to your child in a logical and firm fashion. Also be clear about your expectations for attendance. Your child does not have a choice about attending regular school, and I think he does not need to have a choice about attending Sunday school and most youth activities, even through high school. However, some parents set an age at which a child can begin to choose whether to go or not. Make it clear what age that is.

Other parents say that their children must go to some church activities but may choose another church, perhaps one with more of their friends, if they prefer. So long as what that church teaches is acceptable to you and the transportation problem is not an issue then this might be a good compromise.

However, sometimes refusing Sunday school is just a way a rebellious child can get back at you. Have you caused some hurt in his life that has resulted in resentment and a need to get even? Or are you in a power struggle? If so, try to heal those interpersonal issues and see if the Sunday-school issue disappears.

Also, constructively take a look at your son's class. See if it is the kind of environment that would attract him and make him want to go and gain some profitable experiences there. Help your church make your Sunday school truly worthwhile. There is a great variety of Sunday school curricula, and one of them ought to be right for your son's class. You always help your child when you teach spiritual values, self-discipline, obedience, and respect.

BIG PEOPLE'S CHURCH

We want our preschooler to begin joining us in church on Sundays, since she is too old for the nursery and no junior church is available. So far every attempt has been embarrassing, with lots of whispering, crawling, and distractions. Should we persevere and hope for the best, or wait a while and try again later?

I can still vividly recall feeling bored and as if I absolutely could not sit still for one more minute in church! Fortunately, my parents were quite understanding. My mother had a way with a pencil and paper, and when she realized that I simply could not tolerate one more minute, she would take out that paper and with her pencil create the most marvelous pictures. Then my father would have his turn. In his suit pocket he kept a sack of wintergreen candies. When he knew that I simply could not sit still another minute, he would rustle that paper very softly, and I knew that help was on the way. That paper and piece of candy got me through those endless moments.

Church really is not geared to preschoolers, and perhaps cannot be. What they can learn from adult church is quite limited. I think it's ideal if a children's church or activity time is available. If this is not an option, however, the parents need to train the child to sit still.

If it's necessary for your preschooler to be in church, try going in for a short period of time, then take her outside for a time, and then back in, so that she gradually becomes accustomed to the time and the structure of the service. Gradually increase the child's time to sit still. Use some firmness in requiring a little extra time and attention each week, so the child will increasingly be able to tolerate sitting still.

Also, provide some quiet distractions, such as plastic water-filled toys, activity books, hand-held electronic games with the sound turned off, handicrafts like friendship bracelets and, for older kids, good Christian books. Above all, be careful to keep God's house a place to which you and your child love to go.

■ ■ ■

CHAPTER 13

SOCIAL DEVELOPMENT

GOOD JUDGMENT

How can I teach my child to be discerning, without being too picky or expecting perfection? I'm afraid he may become too rigid—a difficult person to please.

That's an interesting question and one that brings up a very important value in my life. *Discernment* means an ability to evaluate and choose what is best for the people involved. I think discernment is a great gift to have. And it is a quality that can be taught.

Here are some suggestions as to how parents might teach discernment to their children. First, I believe *parents must start with themselves* and their example. Look through your own decision-making methods. How do you decide what is good nutrition for yourself and your family? How do you balance your food intake, the times for your meals, mealtime topics of conversation, the mood, the sense of intimacy that focuses around mealtimes? Discernment can be played out and exemplified in such practical areas. Your choice of friends, your lifestyle decisions, your home atmosphere, your priorities, your work ethic—all of those topics demand good judgment or discernment.

Here are some simple, practical suggestions for teaching a young child to make good choices:.

Give your child limited choices within the framework of his ability to choose, such as having a whole glass or a half glass of juice for breakfast, or whether he wants to wear a green sweatshirt or a blue one with jeans. Compliment your child on those choices that show good taste.

Give the child feedback when he makes choices that are not quite so good. Help him to see how to choose more wisely the next time, without being too critical or condemning. For example, if he made fun of a friend on the playground, help him to see how that friend might have been hurt. Help him to see other ways of solving the same problem.

Tell someone else in the child's hearing about his growing sense of good judgment. These small, daily choices will eventually be translated into good judgment in the more complex, moral areas of life. Good emotional health is evidenced by the decisions we make. Discernment makes such decisions possible, for you and your child.

Raising a Good Future Spouse

What can parents teach their children now about being a good husband or wife?

The characteristics of a good adult, be it husband, wife, or single, start with these qualities:

- The ability to give and receive with generosity and gratitude. Far too often, I find people unable to give, and on the other hand, unable to ask or receive from anyone else. This ability must include giving physical affection as well as material things.
- The ability to be open, honest, and trusting. Real intimacy that is involved in a good relationship within families or within friendships depends upon these qualities. Obviously being open and trusting must be balanced with the development of good judgment. There need to be some areas of privacy, and we don't have to be open to the extent of telling everything we know to everyone.
- The ability to handle loss or disappointment and to grieve with simplicity and sincerity is essential to being a good parent, a good friend, or a good spouse.

- The ability to respect oneself and the other person, to be proud of one another, and to build up one another—to express the pride that we feel *with* one another *to* one another.
- The ability to negotiate, to work through disagreements with respect and love for one another.
- The ability to delay gratification. Being able to hold off on some immediate pleasure in order to gain some higher good later on.

How do you teach these to your little child? First and most importantly, by modeling, by demonstrating these qualities toward one another as mother and father. Second, I think you teach these to your children by sitting down with them now and then and verbally giving them guidelines for how they must get along with one another, as well as with you. Third, through the methods of discipline and training that you employ, you teach your little child to begin developing the qualities that will help him grow up to be a wonderful friend, a good spouse, and a marvelous parent.

AN UNGRATEFUL CHILD

What can parents do to help a child who has established a pattern of being ungrateful?

Some parents have difficulty saying no to their kids. The United States is a culture of affluence. After the Depression of the 1930s and the war of the 1940s, an entire generation of parents wanted their children to have everything they had not been able to enjoy. Meanwhile, science continued to produce new and exciting inventions for pleasure. Motorized toys, talking dolls, video and computer games are all for children's pleasure. Advertising has made all of these things very obvious to children, and the presentation of exciting new items is a daily occurrence on television.

If parents want to break the habit of materialism, here's a system that's certain to cure the problem if parents have the courage to follow it: First, begin by being aware that you have given much to your children.

Second, find ways of showing emotional warmth without gifts. Telling happy jokes, playing a game together, planning an outing that would really be fun—not costly and not sophisticated—can help your children to know that simple happenings can satisfy their cravings.

Third, stop giving gifts, except small, carefully selected ones for very special events. When the child asks for more, explain your new philosophy of giving less and enjoying more what you have.

If your child wants a special item, require him to work and save for it. Give him extra jobs, perhaps, and help him earn money himself. You will find he will be much more appreciative when he has had to sweat to earn it. Require your child to express gratitude and do that yourself. As you teach and model for your child the spirit of gratitude, I think you will find your own joy in life increasing, as well as your pride in your child.

Influences

Who has the greatest influence on a child?

That answer depends upon the family. When parents are really involved in the lives of their children, then *they* are the greatest influence. A recent study has verified that even for rebellious teens, their parents have the greatest influence. Parents must remember this and keep the influence loving, wise, and strong.

But when parents become too busy or involved with other concerns and neglect their children, then other influences come into play. Many people today are concerned about the impact of a child's *friends,* as well as the influence of *teachers* who may not always be very godly people. These are concerns I share. *Television* has an impact on most of us because it is on in our homes so much of the time. If we are not careful and alert, so that we can counteract the messages of the commercials and the programs, then television can powerfully affect our children.

Mothers and fathers can be the most powerful influence in the lives of their children. In the preadolescent period, *mother is generally the major force.* The father is present, and his influence varies with his involvement with the family. Mother's best influence comes in the unique balance of nurturing and guiding—a positive criticalness to discern the problems and dangers in a child's life. Through her womanhood she can help her son understand how to relate to the opposite sex, and she can model femininity and self-respect for her daughter.

Fathers become more influential in the teenage years, though we now know that they are very important in the preschool days as well. The father demonstrates the protection, guidance, and teaching that a male can offer if he is willing to assume that responsibility. His approval and disapproval are very powerful factors in a young person's life. He, too, offers a role model for his son to become a man and for his daughter to relate to men.

SELF-ESTEEM

What can parents do to help a boy or girl who feels insecure?

You can help a child with poor self-esteem in many ways:

- Love unconditionally. Children must be loved for who they are and not for what they do. That acceptance and love should be communicated with absolute honesty. You cannot pretend to love a child and have him believe it. It must be real.
- Discipline firmly, lovingly, and consistently. Your child will learn to be and do the things that are worthy of pride and self-respect.
- Express pride. Tell your child you like what she does and who she is. Be careful to avoid a mixture of approval and disapproval. Never say to a child, "That's fine but…" In my experience the *but* always eliminates the *fine* in the mind of a child. The best

compliments are specific rather than generic. A child will more easily hear and accept, "I love the colors you chose to wear today. You really have an eye for how things go together" rather than "That's a great outfit."

- Be positive. Laugh and play together. When life becomes heavy and is a worry, children lose a very important ingredient in the building of self-esteem. So work at keeping an attitude and atmosphere of congeniality, warmth, and laughter, which, as the Bible so beautifully says, "does good like a medicine."

- Listen to your child. Spend time with your child so that she feels valued. Talk to her about feelings and try to find out if she frequently criticizes herself or berates herself. If she does, try to teach her how to accept her mistakes and forgive herself. If she does not, find out if someone else criticizes her a lot—a parent, grandparent, or neighbor, for instance. Or maybe she feels criticized by you.

- Talk to your child. Share your thoughts, feelings, interests, and desires with your children. This models good communication for them and helps them feel that you value them enough to talk to them about personal things.

- Help your child shine at something. Work at exploring new interests, abilities, and activities. Look for a skill your child can develop further. Then spend time with her and help her develop it. As your child grows in skills that she can share with playmates, you will find that the friendliness automatically happens. Children will crowd around her to learn the exciting new skill that she has mastered.

- Encourage making friends. Help your child with social adjustments. When she finds some new friends, maybe one or two at a time, let her bring them into your home, where you can observe your child and encourage her to play comfortably and successfully.

- Solicit your child's help. Asking her for a back rub or a bit of advice on a perplexing problem will make your child feel that she is making a real contribution and being a big help.
- Seek outside advice. Finally, do not hesitate to seek a counselor to help your child if you believe that she has a serious problem with self-esteem. Sometimes an impartial friend can help a child to feel more confident and valued.

ENEMIES OF SELF-ESTEEM

What are some of the enemies of self-esteem that parents need to guard against?

One of the most important enemies of self-esteem is that of the *parents' negative attitude.* I find a great many parents approach their responsibilities as mother and father by feeling that it's their main job to discover what is wrong with their children and correct it. So be sure that your attitude as parents is positive, and that you look for the strengths more than for the defects.

Another enemy is *chronic marital strife.* A child can hardly feel secure and confident when he daily fears losing one of his parents. When you argue intensely and regularly, children are afraid that one of you may leave.

Discrediting each other as mother and father, finding fault, or criticizing each other in front of the child can also make him feel inadequate. Whether you like it or not, the child will see himself as being like one or the other of you, and criticizing each other indirectly condemns the child. This is a particular problem for divorcing parents, as the ex-spouse often receives a lot of criticism in front of the children. Remember that when you criticize your spouse you are also criticizing your offspring of that spouse.

Be careful to avoid *name calling* in your family. As certainly as you attach a label to your child, he will tend to feel that that's how he must be. That form of destructive criticism is going to destroy a child's self-esteem.

Placing blame is another self-esteem wrecker. When your child has done wrong, he needs to learn confession, restitution, and forgiveness. If he feels guilty, he will believe that he can never be good enough. Avoid discipline that lays shame or guilt. Focus on redemption and learning to be better.

Combining criticism with praise is another self-esteem destroyer. If your spouse constantly said, "I like you, but I wish you were more…" pretty soon you would not remember any of the positive comments. Children need to have discipline and guidance in learning how to act and how to do things, but they need to have that done separately from the praise.

Disapproving of your child's friends is another sure way of hurting his self-esteem, so try very hard to accept those friends and let them enter into your family's life in a positive way. Then your child will know that you approve of his choices. Of course, if certain friends are clearly damaging to your child, you will need to help him discern the problems there.

I hope, parents, that you will avoid these enemies of self-esteem, and that as you develop your own self-confidence as parents you will transmit this to your children.

HEROES

What kind of influence do heroes have?

Many years ago heroes tended to be local people like the family doctor or the mayor. Later, heroes came from books, and the books a child read would provide him with role models. But in today's world the heroes are the well-paid sports stars, weird video musicians, and television celebrities. Some heroes are even characters in television cartoons and sitcoms.

While some sports stars and television personalities are truly good and generous people, the majority are not. They are heroes not because of what they have achieved or what causes they espouse but simply because they are rich celebrities.

A true hero is one who manifests higher values like integrity, generosity, kindness, compassion, honesty, industry, gentleness, love, and faith. A hero is someone who, forgetting his own needs, lives for God and the good of others.

Parents can help children find good heroes by introducing them to high-quality literature, including biographies, renting videos of some of the classics of literature and history, and buying videos that exhibit Christian values. Local libraries often carry children's audiotapes and videotapes that focus on good heroes, such as great musicians of the past or characters in great literature. Public television stations also carry programs that offer children images of truly heroic people of many different races. And Christian bookstores carry a wide range of books and tapes that provide children with superstars who are good models.

You can also teach your child that no one is perfect, even the Christian hero. All of us make mistakes, and good heroes will admit these honestly and ask for forgiveness and restoration.

CHAPTER 14

PHYSICAL AND SEXUAL DEVELOPMENT

SHOES

Do you think it's necessary to buy expensive shoes for children? One of the reasons I've avoided the discount places is because they are self-service, and I'm not really sure how to pick out shoes that fit.

Sometimes better shoes (or more expensive ones) are necessary, yet those times are fairly rare. Most children have such average feet that any shoes are perfectly fine. Those children who have orthopedic problems will demand special fitting. Watch your child's feet, therefore, to see if they tend to toe out or in. Notice the child's ankles as she walks. See if the ankles collapse inward or if the child walks on the outer edge of the foot. If you can't tell that for sure by watching the child walk, notice where the shoes tend to wear. If they wear on the inner sole, then it is possible that the child's ankles or arches are weak. If the outer part wears off sooner, then the child's foot may be rolling outward in a way that can create problems later on. If you have concerns, ask your pediatrician. He or she may refer you to an orthopedic doctor who will decide if the child's feet need special orthotic devices or different shoes. If you are unsure about shoes, certainly go to a shoe store that caters to children and have a well-trained salesperson fit your child's feet.

Otherwise, you can fit your child's shoes yourself. It's best to shop for shoes in the afternoon or evening, when feet may be swollen. When the shoe is on the foot, the child's new shoe should be a *thumb's width too long.* That means that if you press down where the child's big toe is, your thumb should fit between the big toe and the end of the shoe. It should be about *half a finger's width* (or the edge of your finger) *too wide* as you press the edge of your finger between the little toe and the edge of the shoe. You should have enough room to feel that finger settle into leather or fabric at that point. This gives room for your child's foot to spread a little and to grow enough to get reasonable wear out of the shoe without its being so large that it creates blisters or discomfort from friction. When you go to an expensive shoe store with a skilled shoe salesperson, watch how he or she fits your child, and you will learn some of the techniques for buying at least some of your child's shoes in a less-expensive store.

DENTAL CARE

When do parents need to start their children on a dental-care program?

Most parents are told clearly by their pediatrician how often to bring a baby in for check-ups and when to come in for immunizations. If you did not get a schedule of appointments from your doctor when your baby was born, you should ask for one.

On the other hand, few parents are given much direction about dental care. A dentist friend of mine tells me that as soon as a baby's teeth begin to erupt, dental care should begin. Although baby teeth are only temporary, they should still be protected from decay. And this is not hard. Even a child of just a few months can have his teeth swabbed with a soft cotton cloth (no toothpaste) before bed. Milk leaves a film on babies' teeth, and that film encourages the growth of the bacteria that cause tooth decay. That is one reason pediatricians warn parents not to put a child to bed with a bottle of milk or juice. If a child must have a bottle at bedtime, it should be water only.

A child's diet is also very important in providing good tooth development and preventing decay. Too many starches and sugars or highly refined, soft diets leave tiny particles of food in the mouth that promote bacterial growth. Rougher foods that contain whole grains and crusts can help to rub off the film that collects and may prevent some of the particle deposits that cause tooth decay. The old adage "An apple a day keeps the doctor away" works for the dentist as well. Try eating an apple sometime when you've not brushed your teeth. You will find that after you eat that apple, your teeth feel clean and fresh. There is an enzyme in the apple that actually cleans teeth, so to help promote good tooth care give your child plenty of fruit, particularly apples. Don't give raw apples or whole grapes to a baby or toddler, though, because they can cause choking.

Older children should brush their teeth after every meal to remove food particles and to toughen their gums. When they are in school, brushing twice a day is adequate. Use fluoride toothpaste and provide small, soft brushes for plenty of brushing time without hurting the child's gums. Teach them to spit out the toothpaste, not swallow it, as it is not meant for eating!

Flossing a child's teeth is important too. The in-between tooth surfaces certainly are cleaned best with floss.

A child's first visit to the dentist should come somewhere between his second and third birthdays. He can just go along with you on a regular visit or with some other relative who has a relaxed, positive attitude toward dentists. Your child should become familiar with the dentist's office, and the dentist should speak to him personally about dental care. Then when regular visits begin—perhaps about age three—the child will not be afraid of the dentist's office.

CONTACT LENSES

At what age would you consider getting contacts for a child?

That is a problem that I have had to contend with personally, because all of my children wear glasses. My experience is, however, that very few eye doctors will recommend contacts for children younger than twelve to fourteen. Twelve, in fact, is quite early. Soft contacts are safer than the hard ones, but even soft contacts have some risks.

There are several issues that can help parents to know how to choose the time for contacts. First of all, the degree of visual impairment is important, and children who are extremely nearsighted benefit most from contacts. Because contacts go directly over the eyes, the vision is better, the convenience greater, and the child may believe she looks better without glasses.

Another issue to consider is a child's level of responsibility. Contacts take a great deal of care. They can be lost; they are expensive; they must be kept clean in order to avoid infections or injury to the eye. If your child is not very responsible, you may find that neither you nor the child can afford the luxury of contact lenses. Even with great care, contact lenses can cause damage to the cornea of the eye.

A third issue is your child's activity level. Children who are in swimming or other active sports are much more likely to have their contact lenses damaged, lost, or broken. Broken contact lenses in the eye can cause irreparable damage.

A final issue is the degree of social stigma that wearing glasses causes. In earlier grades, wearing glasses can make a child seem more glamorous to her friends or can cause her to be teased. The teasing, however, can usually be dealt with by teaching the child a clever response to offer children who make fun of her. But in the later grades, especially high school, glasses can seriously affect a child's sense of self-esteem.

Ask your eye doctor to recommend the right time and the way your child may move from glasses to contact lenses. Look into insurance policies for contacts during the active, growing-up years when they can be readily lost. Hard contact lenses are often recommended for children whose sight is deteriorating because the hard contacts can slowly reshape the eye. There are even contacts that are worn only a few hours a day that reshape the eye permanently. But these hard contact lenses can also be painful for the child. Many young people cannot tolerate the irritation caused by hard contacts while the eye is getting used to them. If that is the case with your child, discuss the options with your eye doctor. He or she may have many alternatives to suggest, including surgery.

If surgery is suggested, think about getting a second opinion and check out the doctor who suggested the surgery. This is a radical move with serious risks, and you and your child should not go into it lightly or too early in life. Yet some eye clinics present surgery as if it were foolproof. Your child's vision is priceless. Take good care of it.

SPEECH PROBLEMS

How can parents decide if their boy or girl has a speech problem serious enough to merit attention?

Many speech problems of children are temporary. For instance, I heard of a little boy who simply would not talk. The parents came to the doctor repeatedly, asking for help. He checked the boy's palate and tongue and every area of the child's body to find out why he was not talking. He was mentally capable of talking. He was sent to various speech pathologists for a diagnosis and evaluation, and no one could find anything wrong. But when that boy turned six and went to first grade, he began talking and has barely stopped ever since!

One speech concern, then, is that of *delayed speech*. When a child has reached three or four years of age and is not talking, parents need to wonder. Medical professionals do not worry about a speech delay until that time, however, because some children simply do not talk much before then. If the child shows other evidence of problems, such as not responding when spoken to, then a checkup is required to rule out a hearing problem.

The second speech concern is *abnormal sounds*. The child who lisps and pronounces *s* as if it is *th,* or who confuses *r* and *l* as well as other sounds, will cause his parents to worry. Many abnormal sounds are related to hearing baby talk from parents, even when the child is no longer small. Most children will outgrow this habit when adults routinely stop the baby talk. My speech pathologist consultant says that parents need not worry about abnormal sounds until eight or nine years of age. If the baby sounds persist through that time, a speech therapist should evaluate the child. Most public schools provide well-qualified speech therapists, so take advantage of this resource.

Stuttering and stammering is a serious condition that worries many people. A friend of mine indicated that his boy began stammering so badly he could not get a sentence out. He and his wife took the child to a speech pathologist. As the pathologist worked with them and the little boy, she discovered that the child, being the youngest of the family, was not able to get anyone's attention when he wanted to talk. So he learned to stutter in order to keep the center stage once he did get it! Despite doubting that this was the problem, the family followed her recommendation, which was to give the child plenty of time to talk and plenty of attention. He overcame his difficulty very quickly.

A refusal to speak because of anger or fear is not uncommon. We call that *elective mutism*. If that is to be corrected, both the child and the parents must have the help of a professional.

Almost all children learn to talk. They may talk too much or too little. They may talk with a little difficulty, but the important fact for you to remember is that communicating the love and concern you feel is what really counts.

CHECKPOINTS FOR SEX EDUCATION

What attitudes about sex should children have learned by the time they reach school age?

There are six attitudes in all, and they begin with the parents.

1. Good body image. A child's attitude toward her body is an important element in sexuality. If the child feels that the sexual parts of her body are shameful, and she is embarrassed by them, then she will come to marriage later on with inhibitions and misconceptions that can make her sexual relationship unhappy. Teach your child that *her body is beautiful,* that God made it, and that she needs to value it and give it dignity and pride. Of course, not being ashamed does not mean that a child flaunts her body or exposes herself to others.

2. *Open attitude.* Children need to have an *open, accepting, and honest attitude toward sex.* That attitude, parents, comes from you. I have worked with many families in which the parents were so ashamed to talk about sexuality that the child could not have an open, unashamed attitude. You need to talk with one another, read wholesome books, and share your ideas with trusted friends until you become comfortable with your feelings about sexuality.

3. *Accurate information.* I find many families do not have a vocabulary with which to discuss sexual issues. You need to learn the *names for the various parts of the body,* as well as their functions. Any junior-high health textbook or encyclopedia can provide those.

4. *Respect for privacy.* Teach your child to *respect the privacy* of others and expect it in return. Many children investigate one another's bodies out of curiosity, but this can result in exploring that frightens the child. You need to teach your child not only to respect, admire, and appreciate her own body, but to respect others' privacy as well.

5. *Respect for self.* Your child also deserves privacy and dignity. Her *body is her own,* and no one has the right to touch it without her permission. Most schools now have a program called "Good Touch, Bad Touch" that helps children distinguish between loving touches and touches that violate their privacy

and lead to sexual abuse. Reinforce this teaching at home so your child will not be exploited.

6. *Awe of God's creation.* Teach your child to *approach the human body with awe* for God's creation. The "bottom line" of all these attitudes is that sexuality and the human body are God's creations, and they were created to be good.

FAMILY NUDITY

Do you think there is any harm in having my two-year-old daughter and her seven-year-old brother take their baths together? And what about letting them in the room when their dad and I are dressing or bathing?

Parents need to keep an emphasis on naturalness when young children bathe together. Sexuality, and male and female bodies, are gifts from God to be appreciated and protected. Children should not be taught to feel shame about their naked bodies. But they should be taught that their bodies are their own, not to be touched or exploited by anyone.

Bathing children together can be a neat way to allow them to see the boy/girl differences. However, as a parent, you ought to be present when children bathe together in order to prevent an unwholesome preoccupation with the sexual parts of their bodies. If they ask questions about the differences between them, calmly explain them. And comply promptly when a child asks to begin to bathe privately.

The question of whether children should see their parents unclothed is a common one. Many parents go around the house without much on in the presence of their children. This has had no harmful effect whatsoever. On the other hand, if parents do not normally do this, then a child may express surprise if he suddenly comes upon a scantily dressed parent. Take your cue from your child. If it bothers the child, then I suggest that you practice privacy. In today's sexually focused culture, I tell parents to weight their decisions toward privacy.

TOUCHING MOMMY

My four-year-old has become interested in my breasts—both when I am undressed and when I am clothed. I don't want her to think of this as ugly or forbidden, and yet I don't want her interest to continue. She saw me breastfeeding over a year ago and was not at all interested then.

Many three- and four-year-olds develop an interest in Mommy's breasts. In my experience, this almost always relates to a time that they have seen their mother or another mother nursing a baby. Even though this was a year ago, the child would not have forgotten that experience, and there may be some special reason why she is renewing her interest now.

Frankly, I see this as a natural curiosity. It gives parents a wonderful chance to explain the purpose of a mother's breasts and ask for any questions she may have about Mother's body. A little girl may be curious about why she is a girl and yet she doesn't have breasts. Explain to her that someday she will develop breasts, and help her to know how and when that will happen. With either a boy or a girl, it is important to recognize that you know they like the feel of soft things, and being a soft mommy is part of the cuddling that all children and parents enjoy. Explain frankly, however, that you do not feel comfortable being touched or stroked on that part of your body—either alone or in front of other people.

EFFEMINATE SON

I'm getting worried about my ten-year-old son. I've caught him dressing up in my women's clothes, and he seems to thoroughly enjoy it. Am I overreacting? Can you help me know what to do?

Many boys dress up in girls' or women's clothing at times, such as at Halloween. That is quite a different issue than the one addressed by this mother. This mom is concerned about her son's habitual preference for feminine items. This can lead to a problem when the child reaches puberty and is searching for a sexual identity.

In dealing with this concern, first make sure you have a loving, happy relationship with your son. Sometimes children dress in their parents' clothes in order to feel close to them. Is there a chance that your son is seeking a closer relationship with you?

Second, I would make sure that he has access to some soft, silky men's shirts. He may just enjoy the texture of your clothes. Or perhaps he does not have access to men's clothes. Allow him to dress up in Daddy's clothes, or get him some hand-me-downs from adult male friends. Let him try out the big shoes, hats, jackets, or shirts.

Third, ensure that your son spends time with men and boys. Have Dad take time to teach him what he does at work. Have your son help Dad clean the car or the family room, mow the grass, go fishing, cook, do the laundry, or whatever Dad does. Make sure that he has male friends that he enjoys.

If Dad is not an active part of your son's life, check whether he has a warm, positive relationship with some other significant male. Include in your family activities other male relatives or adult friends who can be good role models for him. So long as this man is respectful of your son, affirming, and never abusive or intrusive, you should encourage the relationship and make sure your son has time to see this friend.

Do not punish or disapprove of your son's effeminacy. That will drive it into hiding and cause guilt and fear. He may be afraid that he is different from other boys and that something is wrong with him. As his mother, you need to understand his needs for approval, closeness, warmth, and softness.

Avoid overreacting. Simply encourage masculinity in your son. Teach him to open doors for you and to carry things for you. Be proud of his masculine traits, and reflect them to him in compliments. Connect him with boys who share his interests but are not so effeminate. Find ways to turn his effeminate tendencies into sensitive masculinity. Your son can grow in his own unique way into manhood, and you can be very proud of him.

DAD NEEDED

I'm a single parent, and my two girls do not see their father much due to distance and his ongoing problems. How important is it for them to be close to a dad?

Dads are vitally important in the lives of both boys and girls. Girls need Dad's pride and delight in them if they are to have the healthy sense of self-worth they need. When Dad is involved in her life, a girl is significantly more likely to be motivated and successful in school, sports, and just about any other aspect of her life. Furthermore, it is through Dad's example that she learns about men and how to love and respect them, and how to choose a good husband if she decides to marry.

A child who does not have an involved father would benefit from building a close relationship with another adult male. This could be Grandpa or an uncle, or it could be a friend or neighbor. Be sure that the man is respectful of her affection, positive, and never abusive nor intrusive, and that male friend can be a valuable adopted member of the family.

DELAYED OR EARLY PUBERTY

What are the worries for a teen who may mature either earlier or later than his or her peers?

The preadolescent and adolescent years can be difficult, even under the best of circumstances. That difficulty can be multiplied for the boy or girl whose biological clock is a bit off from the majority. Any differences certainly carry their own set of problems.

Early or late puberty is more obvious in girls because of their breast development (or lack thereof) and menstrual cycles. Girls who develop as early as ten or eleven commonly feel as if they have been unfairly pushed into an adult world for which they feel unprepared. They feel different from their peers and almost have a sense of being abused. Young girls become embarrassed when they have their periods. If they have an accident in school, they do not know how to handle it. They need help from parents and teachers to prevent such accidents and to protect their privacy.

Some people believe that early puberty causes an early preoccupation with sexual interests, but I disagree. Sexual awareness is an issue, and one that demands consideration by parents to prevent a child's precocious or excessive fascination with sexual interests. But early puberty does not necessarily equate with early sexual interest. The point is that the early-developing child will need protection from the sexual advances of those who think she is older than she really is and support in dealing with peers who treat her differently because of her early development.

Girls who develop late will also face consequences, especially if their chests remain flat when all their peers are sporting filled-out bras. Such a girl may struggle with poor self-esteem and may have to put up with some cruel jokes or teasing, especially in gym class. Like any child with an unusual characteristic, this girl should be taught to respond flippantly and proudly to those who make fun of her, thereby letting the wind out of the sails of her teasers. Something like "Did you know that _____ (plug in the name of the latest supermodel) did not wear a bra till she was much older?" could stop the comments and communicate that this flat-chested girl is not to be tangled with.

Boys, too, may be late bloomers. And they have as much of a problem as the girls who find the advent of their puberty early. Boys who remain short, whose voices do not change as soon as their friends, who do not develop hair growth and other signs of masculinity with their friends, often feel left out, inadequate, different, and can develop a serious inferiority complex. Again, you might want to help your son by looking up facts about famous athletes who were (or are) short and giving him this as ammunition to use if attacked by teasers.

Boys who develop early tend not to face as many consequences as girls who develop early because the boys' puberty is not so easily recognized. Boys who are tall and manly tend to receive more respect than their younger-seeming peers. However, these boys may struggle to accept their sexual feelings, becoming embarrassed by wet dreams and aroused desires. Boys need to be taught by their parents that these events are normal and expected.

If you believe that your child is not developing normally, have him or her examined and let your doctor decide whether there is a hormonal imbalance or other need for concern. If your child is concerned, the physician can reassure him or her. Don't let your child feel different or inadequate because of his or her particular clockwork. Instead, if your child wants to compensate, help him or her to dress and groom in a way that will make up for the differences in development and enable the child to fit better into the social sphere of peers.

SEXUAL PEER PRESSURE

In your counseling, do you see teenagers who are feeling pressure to be sexually active?

It's a sad fact that many teenagers become sexually active quite early. Teenage pregnancies are extremely common, and sexually transmitted diseases are epidemic. Whether we like to admit it or not, even teens from "good" families are not insulated from pressures to be sexually active. They can be made to feel almost abnormal if they are not as experienced as their classmates. One study revealed that over 45 percent of regularly churched youth have had sex before completing high school.

A very good friend of mine happens to be a teacher, and she came home from school one day to find her own eighth-grade daughter in a risky situation with a young man she was dating. When my friend talked with her daughter about this and what could have happened, the child said, "But, Mother, I'm the only one of my friends who has never had sex." I think it was sad that a fourteen-year-old should have to say that, but it was true.

Peers are very important to adolescents. I find a great many children (and literally they are "old" children) feeling lonely. Out of their loneliness, they have a need for companionship that very quickly can become physical rather than just social. One girl I worked with some years ago felt that because she was so lonely, she owed anyone who paid her any attention—even the purchase of a soft drink after school—a sexual favor in return.

The push of young people into premature adulthood is common today. There's too much information available to young people much too soon. There is too little comfortable openness with parents. Talking about questions and feelings and finding thoughtful answers within the family is not very common. There is far too much exposure to sexually stimulating sights and ideas on television and in magazines. Local grocery stores or drugstores often display explicit materials on open shelves, available to anyone.

The recreational attitude about sex—that it's simply something for fun—detracts from this very beautiful, significant part of life.

I suggest that parents forbid real "dating" until at least age fifteen. By then teens have developed some self-awareness and a degree of maturity. Talk *with* them (not *at* them) about establishing wholesome dating practices focused on healthy activities. While recognizing their feelings, help them identify ways to avoid sexually stimulating places while controlling sexual impulses. Keep an open, nonjudgmental, interested but not controlling attitude, and your teens will be open with you.

There are a number of groups (such as True Love Waits) that are promoting celibacy and the saving of sex for marriage. A few contemporary Christian musicians and athletes also encourage purity. And many churches sponsor youth groups that aim to help young people resist sexual temptation and encourage them to conduct their social lives in groups instead of couples. Teens will benefit from finding friends who share their values and beliefs and who will not treat them as weirdos if they are not sexually active. Help your teen to find those friends and offer him or her the means to socialize with them.

PLASTIC SURGERY

If you could afford to give your child either a better education or a better-looking face, which would you choose?

I am assuming here that the question is being asked about a child with a truly disfiguring flaw. I definitely believe that a better education will benefit a child more than a handsome face or a sexually appealing body. Becoming a productive person offers much more meaning and purpose in life than having a good appearance.

Therefore, if you are asking about surgery simply to reduce a large nose or sharpen a weak chin, then I believe you ought to ask yourselves some questions. Who is it that judges whether a child's appearance is good or bad? Sometimes, because of certain familial traits or values, parents can be overly sensitive about certain aspects of appearance. For example, if you were teased about your nose as a child, you will be especially sensitive to your son's feelings if he has the same nose. Also, different cultures look for different types of beauty. In the U.S., we might think a child's nose too big or the jaw too small. Yet in parts of Europe a large nose is often seen as a sign of distinction. So, you need to think about whether your child's problem is a real one or one that's related to family or community values.

Further, parents ought to examine how abnormal their child really is in comparison with his or her friends. Is the child feeling inferior or inadequate because of a characteristic or a handicap that may be corrected? It is rare, in my experience, to find children who are so unusual that they stand out as being ugly. Offering plastic surgery to a child who simply has a bony nose or flatter breasts or stringier muscles than some communicates to that child that she is not good enough as she is and needs to be "fixed." She will spend her life in search of the perfect body rather than searching for happiness where it can be found—in her faith, her family, and God's world.

If your child does have a significant disfigurement, such as scarring from burns or a prominent birthmark, let me suggest what you may do for your child:

- Go to a physician and talk about the issue. Is surgery recommended? How much will it cost? Is it possible that by having a psychiatric evaluation and determining how seriously the problem affects your child's emotional health that your insurance may cover the cost of plastic surgery?
- Is there a nonsurgical way to correct the problem? Many children can enhance their appearance by cosmetic means, such as getting a new haircut, wearing a certain type of clothing, or, as they get older, wearing contact lenses or corrective makeup.

If corrective procedures are impossible or you cannot afford to have them done, then you need to help your child to understand that this disfigurement is part of what makes him or her unique. It is something that will cause some grief, but the child can get through that grief and move on to understanding that appearances are not all there is. As your child learns to compensate for limits in one area, he or she will develop a greater sense of strength in other areas. Developing academic skills, social skills, and activities that can be shared with other children can more than compensate for the heartache of having a significantly flawed appearance. Teach your child to use her own pain to learn compassion for others. And teach your child that all of us, to each other and to God, are beautiful when we are beautiful on the inside. Even the most glamorous model is ugly when the heart is full of evil.

THE MOTHERS'
QUESTIONNAIRE

This Mothers' Questionnaire was completed by nearly five hundred women from coast to coast. Perhaps you would like to take it too. To compare your results with the collated national sampling, see Survey Results.

MOTHERS' QUESTIONNAIRE

I am writing a book which will give mothers a better understanding of themselves and their children, as well as help mothers to change certain negative behavior patterns. In order to complete the research, I need your assistance. Please answer the following questions. Your anonymous responses are greatly appreciated. Thank you for your time.

—Pat Holt

1. The ages of my children are:_____
2. Screaming at my children is a problem for me
   ❑ Almost Always ❑ Sometimes ❑ Occasionally ❑ Never
3. I am most likely to scream when (please give an appropriate example):

4. I am least likely to scream when:

5. I scream at my children when (please number in order of relevance):
   _____ I am pre-menstrual
   _____ I am frustrated with them
   _____ They just won't listen
   _____ I am tired
   _____ They are irresponsible
   _____ I am under a lot of pressure

_____ They talk back

_____ I've told them 1000 times

_____ Too much is happening at once

_____ I'm angry

6. How do you feel after you scream? (Please give an example.)

7. I scream at my children because (please number in order of relevance):

    _____ It's the only reaction I know

    _____ I hope that volume will drive my message home

    _____ It makes me feel better

    _____ Maybe they will understand how much their behavior affects me

    _____ It's better than hitting them

    _____ Nobody ever taught me how to deal with misbehavior

    _____ It gets results

    _____ It gets their attention

8. How do your children react to your screaming? (Please give an example.)

9. What do you think is an alternative to screaming? (Please explain your answer.)

OPTIONAL INFORMATION

10. Age group:
    ❑ Under 30   ❑ 30 to 39   ❑ Over 39

11. Highest grade level completed:
    ❑ High School   ❑ College Credit   ❑ College Degree   ❑ Graduate Credit
    ❑ Graduate Degree

12. Currently employed?
    ❑ No   ❑ Yes (# of hours per week:_____)

13. Average yearly combined family income:
    ❑ Under $35,000   ❑ $35,000 to $75,000   ❑ Over $75,000

Although responses are anonymous, if you are available for further comment, please include your name, address, telephone number, and best time to call.

On behalf of mothers and children everywhere, thank you.

SURVEY RESULTS

1. Of those surveyed, 16% had only one child; 34% had two children; 34% had three children; and 16% had four or more children. Of those surveyed, 17% had children who were two years old or younger; 24% had children who were between three and five years old; 25% had children in the six- to nine-year-old bracket; 15% had children in the ten-to-twelve age bracket; and 19% had children who were thirteen or older.

2. Of those surveyed, 45% said screaming was sometimes a problem for them; 6% said they almost always screamed at their kids; 43% said they occasionally had problems with screaming; and 6% said they never screamed.

3. The top three answers were (a) when stress becomes too great; (b) when there are too many demands on my limited time; and (c) when I don't feel well.

4. The top four answers were (a) when I am rested; (b) when things are calm; (c) when the children cooperate without complaining; and (d) when I feel I am getting things done.

5. I feel like screaming at my children when (numbered in order from the most frustrating experience to the least frustrating) (1) I am under a lot of pressure; (2) too much is happening at once; (3) I am tired; (4) I've told them a thousand times; (5) they just won't listen; (6) I am frustrated with them; (7) I'm angry; (8) I am premenstrual; (9) they are irresponsible; (10) they talk back.

6. The top four answers were (a) guilty; (b) ashamed or embarrassed; (c) better (I released the tension); and (d) a sense of power.

7. I scream at my children because (numbered in order from the most common reason to the least common reason) (1) it gets their attention; (2) I hope the volume will drive my message

home; (3) it gets results; (4) maybe they will understand how much their behavior affects me; (5) it makes me feel better; (6) it's better than hitting them; (7) it's the only reaction I know; (8) nobody ever taught me how to deal with misbehavior.

8. The top four ways children react to screaming are (a) sadness and hurt feelings; (b) angry back talk; (c) fear and withdrawal; and (d) humiliation and shame.

9. Of those surveyed, 72% felt the best alternative to screaming was to calm down first, then talk to the kids; 23% felt mothers should give firm and loving discipline; and 5% felt that spanking was the alternative.

10. Of the mothers surveyed, 6% were under thirty; 65% were in the thirty to thirty-nine age group; and 19% were over thirty-nine. The rest did not reveal their ages.

11. Of those surveyed, 8% had only high school diplomas; 42% had some college credit; 33% had completed their college degree; and 17% had also done some graduate work.

12. Of the mothers surveyed, 40% were not employed outside the home. Of the 60% who were employed, 15% worked ten hours a week outside the home, 15% worked fifteen hours a week, 28% worked twenty hours a week, and 42% worked full-time (forty hours a week).

Note: It is significant that the women in our study were not aware of how much they screamed until they filled out our Mothers' Questionnaire. A large percentage have told us that just being conscious of their screaming has already helped them to control themselves better. We hope that this encouraging by-product of reading this book will be a large step toward control for you.

INDEX

HG